Abner Haynes

An American Hero

By King David Haynes

Copyright © 2024 King David Haynes

All rights reserved. No part of this book may be reproduced or transmitted in any form or by any means, electronic or mechanical, including photocopying, recording or by any information storage and retrieval system without written permission from the author.

Published by King David Haynes

ISBN-979-8-218-56632-6

Dedication

In memory of my Father Abner Haynes,

a true warrior who made this world a better place.

Rest in peace, Dad

Acknowledgements

I would like to thank my Sister in Christ ArLena Richardson. She has been very generous with her expertise, time, and advice. She is a very accomplished professional who has helped me immensely in my own life. A true friend of the Haynes family.

A very special thanks to Joyce M. Sanders for all of her assistance in presenting this book.

I'd also like to thank my brother Abner Haynes Jr. He has been there for me through thick and thin. His support has been greatly appreciated.

Table of Contents

Foreword 1

Preface 5

Chapter 1: Denton Texas 12

Chapter 2: Lincoln High School 21

Chapter 3: 1956 26

Chapter 4: Integration 30

Chapter 5: First Practice 36

Chapter 6: Corsicana Texas 48

Chapter 7: The Varsity Years 63

Chapter 8: The Hunts 82

Chapter 9: The Pros 92

Chapter 10: The Zale Influence 111

Epilogue 116

About The Author 121

Foreword

It is a profound honor to introduce this book written by King David Haynes, son of the legendary Abner Haynes. My connection to this project goes far beyond my professional role; it is deeply personal. I first caught Abner's attention on Facebook, where he noticed my work as a Black woman striving to make a mark in the sports industry by serving retired professional athletes. Abner admired my consistency, determination, and accomplishments and decided to reach out, knowing that by allowing me to become his publicist, he could help advance my career.

What started as a professional alliance soon blossomed into a profound connection. Abner mentored me and became a father figure, sharing his life experiences of breaking color barriers in sports, his time as a sports agent, his advocacy for civil rights, and his corporate career. Through our numerous phone conversations, he imparted wisdom that only a life as impactful as his could offer.

As our bond deepened, Abner's concern for my personal life grew. Noting my lack of siblings, children, or a husband, he took it upon himself to introduce me to his son, King David, hoping he would become a brotherly figure in my life. Abner desired to ensure I had a family who could offer support and companionship. It didn't take long for King David and me to form a close relationship, which we further solidified by launching a podcast called Slaying Your Giants.

Abner's love for his sons was evident in every story he shared with me, and it was clear that he had poured much of himself into King David. King David speaks, thinks, acts like his father, and carries forward his father's legacy with great pride and care. I was privileged to witness firsthand the closeness between Abner and King David, especially during the latter years of Abner's life. It was truly inspiring to see how King David and his brother Abner, Jr. managed to serve as their father's caregivers while juggling their demanding careers in the oil industry.

King David has shared many unique stories about his experiences as Abner's son, providing a perspective only he could offer. In his book, *Abner Haynes: An American Hero*, King David brings to life the remarkable journey of his father, allowing readers to feel as if they are right there with him, seated at the dinner table, listening to intimate and profound stories. The narrative flows between moments of quiet reflection and lively conversation, capturing the essence of Abner's character and the depth of his impact on those around him. This unique perspective will surely leave you wanting to delve deeper into the book.

Abner Haynes lived with purpose and intention, and he wanted the stories and experiences of his life to resonate beyond his accomplishments. He knew the power of sharing one's journey and the importance of leaving a legacy that others could learn from and be inspired by. Whether you are a family member, friend, colleague, or fan, you will find in these pages a side of Abner that few have seen—a man who left a piece of his humanity with everyone he met.

As you read this book, I hope you feel the warmth and wisdom Abner so generously shared with me and many others. His life was a testament to courage, resilience, and love, and his legacy continues through the words of his son, King David. Together, they remind us that the most significant victories are not just those won on the field but those that bring us closer to understanding and compassion for one another. Abner's legacy is a source of inspiration that will surely uplift anyone who reads this book.

ArLena Richardson, founder of The ArLena Richardson Agency (ArLena.com), has been at the forefront of marketing and management for over three decades, representing some of America's most celebrated retired professional and Olympic athletes, including the renowned Abner Haynes. She holds a Bachelor of Science in Economics from Southern Methodist University and a Master of Business Administration in Information Technology from Western International University. She is on the heels of earning a doctorate in sports management at the United States Sports Academy. Richardson's creativity and passion are evident in her work, having designed an award-winning limited edition sneaker, the Ron Freeman 43.2, to honor the 1968 Olympic gold and bronze medalist. In 2021, she launched her highly praised limited edition handcrafted Italian leather sneaker, PROVEN (proven.luxurybrand.shoes).

Preface

Much has been written and said about my father, Abner Haynes, before he asked me to tell his story from my own perspective. Dad knew that for many years now, he had explained to me what happened, how it happened and who was involved. He knew that I've even had the honor of knowing many of the men and women who were so pivotal in the successful integration of the university systems in the south. There are other writings, awards and honors concerning Abner Haynes that attempt to tell the story of integration in Texas. Dad knew there would be those who read this book that already know some of the facts of his extraordinary life. He also knew that younger fans may not have had the opportunity to see him play. Many younger people have never even heard his name, let alone know the story. It was very important to him for me to tell his story once again for those who can gain inspiration and encouragement in their own lives from seeing the obstacles and stumbling blocks he overcame. There is no denying Dad was a great football player. His name is forever on Arrowhead Stadium in Kansas City, as he is a member of the Chiefs Hall of Fame.

You can find all of his statistics and Hall of Fame memberships elsewhere; this book is to give special insights on the man who changed so much in this country. I have known his fans and former teammates all my life. We have learned and grown from their points of view. Even though Dad began telling me all of this when I was a young kid, I began to understand the significance of his actions and the achievements at North Texas State University (now known as The University of North Texas - used interchangeably throughout this book) as I got older. In walking through our own lives, we know there are many young people who missed Dad's playing years. They don't know anything about all of this. That is the impetus for me presenting this book. The only world they have ever known has been an integrated one, like me. Young people have always been so very important to Dad. His hope was to bring his story to younger fans who weren't around to know how we all got to this point, where anyone can be anything that his talent and effort will allow him to be. We wanted to give life to, and a fresh look at, some of the wonderful episodes and stories throughout his life that my father told me himself over the years.

My Dad asked me to tell you about those that helped mold him into the man he became. He would like to recognize and honor those who gave him so much, which set him on a successful path. At key points throughout his journey, there were unusual men and women involved who made a tremendous difference in Dad's life. It is my heartfelt desire to expand upon what my Dad, Abner's friends and fans already know about him. He did so much for so many. He was an icon in the world of sport and a hero to many others as a trailblazer who helped immensely in the positive racial transformations that occurred in this country. One who — when life and opportunity tested him by being the

"First" in so many areas — was prepared and motivated, which equaled success.

I write this book as a celebration of my father's remarkable life. Abner Haynes passed away on July 17th 2024 at 86 years old. His service was absolutely beautiful. As we greeted and had occasion to talk with the people who were in attendance, I got a fresh sense of who my father was as a young man. Individuals told me their own personal stories about their encounters with Abner Haynes. One in particular I will share. This man was a student and a very good track & field athlete who was attending Lincoln High School in Dallas, my Dad's high school. His family were also members of our church. He told me how my Dad was playing for the Dallas Texans at the time but he would take time out to encourage this young high school athlete and worked with him on his technique on the track. He spoke of the day he and his family, his mom, a single parent with five children in the early 1960's, had no food in the house. He told me while he was sitting there wondering what they were going to do to feed his younger siblings he looked up and saw a big Cadillac coming down the street. It was Abner Haynes. What struck him as so unusual was this was a Sunday morning and Abner had a professional football game to play in a few hours. He told me my Dad had the car full of groceries, including a trunk full of food. That's the kind of man he was. Since elementary school, I have memories of the commitment and passion of my father's fans. Even when I was in the Army in Muenster, Germany, my company commander was from El Paso Texas and saw my Dad play in the 1959 Sun Bowl as a college senior. As I have spoken with his college teammates over the years, the one constant that all mentioned was Abner's infectious spirit and his determination which naturally drew people to him. Starting as a young man he affected people positively all along his journey through this life. Rest in Peace Dad.

Dad lived an exceptional and unique life that touched many.

I can recall being 12 or 13 years old when Dad took us on a road trip like he often did. We drove from Texas to Tampa, Florida for what used to be called the Tangerine Bowl. This is after his pro football career, when he became one of the first Black Sports Agents. Dad had a client named Phillip Dokes from Oklahoma State whom we were there to support. The memories of this legendary trip in my mind had nothing to do with football. My Dad was in the process of teaching us how to drive. My brother Abner Haynes Jr. nor I were new to driving, we had been practicing back at home for a while. We had just entered the state of Florida and were on a small highway as my brother was driving and Dad was in the front seat instructing. We were in a large van that had a bed in the back on which I was lying across, looking out of the big back window. All of a sudden as I looked out the window, I could see we were over a large swamp. The railing of the bridge we were on was only a few inches away. This made me look up and out the front windshield. It may have been the longest bridge I had ever seen and only two lanes. I must admit I was nervous, as I saw the line of 18 wheelers coming at us as the night fell. There were just inches to spare on either side. Dad spoke calmly to Abner Jr., reminding him that he had experience driving and reassuring him that he could do this. None of us knew this bridge was coming up and none of us were ready for it. No one panicked however and my brother held steady and true as he passed this test with flying colors. After making it to Tampa we stayed in a hotel with a huge lake on the grounds. The hotel had all that a fisherman needs right there to use. My brother and I fished all day it seemed. We caught a few fish which the hotel would cook for us. I was having the time of my life, not knowing anything about the business that was going on. I was just with my Dad, Mother and Brother. My Father gave us this wonderful memory instead of leaving us at home. He would spend the extra money so that we all could experience life and grow together.

Upon driving back to Texas, we stopped on a beach somewhere near Mobile, Alabama and camped out for the night right there in Dad's well-equipped van. This was in the 1970s. You could stop like that back in those days without danger you might face now. We opened the side door and took in the sunset on that beach in Alabama while having fresh shrimp and crawfish. It was beautiful, as I remember the look of the sun going down over the ocean — it was like a painting. I thank Dad for giving me these kinds of experiences and memories to hold onto, of which there were many. I thought I was special. I knew we were doing things other kids my age were not. I didn't know what it all meant then but these memories comfort me in times of trial to this day.

Another of the legendary road trips went the other direction. We drove from Dallas to Los Angeles. I was going to the 9th grade I believe and we were going out there for my sister Venita's high school graduation ceremony. We also had many relatives who lived all over California. There was so much excitement and growing up on this trip. Times were different; my brother and I both took turns driving on the Santa Monica Freeway as our sister gave us a tour of the area. I've always loved California for what it is. My sister directed us to a beach there in Santa Monica so we opened the side doors and started playing some music. In about 20 minutes we had a full-scale party going on with people none of us even knew. It was a great trip. Of course, Dad's coming was huge for the California Haynes family, and our relatives out there didn't disappoint. Later that night they had a very large party for us at our cousin's house in the Crenshaw District and I saw Dad relax in a way that was new to me. He was really having a great time. I had never been to a real party with him and certainly had never seen him dance. But with all the trials life presents us all it did something really cool for me to see my father let his guard down so to speak and enjoy himself with his family. He was dancing and laughing, pure joy displayed on his face that I will never forget. I wasn't totally aware of all the things he went through in his life at that point but he felt comfortable and he really could dance. My cousin Wayne was with us as well as Abner Jr. It was a phenomenal trip that we all relived many times until this day. It was one of the happiest weeks of my life. I went to my first nightclub on this trip. I almost felt like I was grown up. I always appreciated that in him. Dad would put us out there because he knew that kids needed experiences to grow.

All my life, I have met random people at the doctor's office, grocery store or somewhere else mundane, who tell me their story of how they were ten years old when their own fathers took them to see Abner Haynes play for the Dallas Texans at the Cotton Bowl or the Kansas City Chiefs. They never forgot him because Dad stopped and signed an autograph or took a picture with them. The fan telling me this would be a grown man, usually older than me, but that person has kept that autograph and cherishes it to this day. People send football cards and helmets in the mail even now for Dad to sign. I can tell from my own experiences with his fans that Dad was very good with them; he would take time with young kids and they never forgot him for it. I am very proud of my father and all that he accomplished despite the times he lived through which ensured the odds were stacked heavily against him.

So, let's dive into some of the wonderful episodes and stories of my father, Abner Haynes' life that he told me himself for years.

Chapter 1:
Denton Texas

Abner Haynes Sr. was born in Denton, Texas on September 19, 1937 to my Grandparents Bishop F.L. Haynes and Ola Mae Haynes. My Dad was the youngest of seven children with four older brothers who were all good athletes. We spent so many hours discussing and remembering his childhood growing up in Denton. I was always fascinated by history so I enjoyed hearing about life from another time. I am so thankful that we talked so much about the people, places and what happened. Most of these crucial players have passed on now, but they still live through our memories and stories about them.

Like kids everywhere, the Haynes kids spent hours playing sports in their neighborhood. They called it East Denton. Dad was raised across the street from the city park on Bailey Street. He would always tell me how all but maybe two people who lived on their street weren't family. They had uncles and aunts on both sides of their house, so all had a hand in raising and supporting each other's families. It was truly a village where the people worked together for the betterment of all. It was a different world then. Segregation was the rule of the day. The family was much tighter back then as all black people in any given city or town were always clustered together in the undesirable part of town. You didn't have the freedom to live anywhere you could afford. That would come later. Due to this fact, families could maintain relationships and assist each other because they all lived in close proximity to each other in the black part of town. Although we cherish the freedom and advancements in the country, I can see just from my own family that with the freedom also came the spreading out of the family. No longer are the Haynes' only in Southeast Denton where you could easily visit all. Today we are all over Texas, California, and Colorado primarily and see each other much less than my father's generation did.

My Dad would tell me how he was the youngest but they wouldn't take any mercy on him. He had four older brothers who were all good athletes themselves. Even the girls played football and were good athletes. Dad told me how his oldest sister Aunt Chee was one of the toughest players in the neighborhood for a couple years. So, from a tender age, his athletic prowess began to be developed right there in Denton. He was always playing sports against girls and boys who were older than him. I think that was a key in developing his athletic gifts. By the time he got to high school, he was already rougher and stronger than others his age.

There is no story that would be complete regarding how Abner was able to accomplish so much without mentioning his father, the late Bishop F.L. Haynes. My grandfather, Bishop Haynes, began to preach the word of God at a young age. At 17 years old, he left his family in Leon County, Texas to establish the first

Holiness church in Denton. He had an aunt who lived there already and felt called to that specific area to preach the word by God. He arrived in Denton, rented a room and got to work. We called him PapaDad. Shortly after settling in Denton, PapaDad had become friends with a white pastor, Reverend John Boone of Sanger, Texas. It is one of those legendary family stories of how my grandfather and Reverend Boone walked the twenty miles from Denton to Sanger to buy a tent which would serve as my grandfather's first church. These two committed men of God walked twenty miles to buy the tent, then on the return trip carried the tent, poles and stakes the twenty miles back to Denton and erected the tent on Robinson St. PapaDad began right there with that tent. He would preach there daily and his tenacity, discipline and spirit started to win souls for the Lord. The church continued to grow and expand as new members joined. Despite the inherent unfairness of life for black people at the time, the church was an oasis where people found stability, peace and purpose through choosing to follow the Godly path.

BISHOP F.L. HAYNES

PapaDad was a spiritual giant. From that humble beginning, God raised up a true warrior. Bishop F.L. Haynes was a serious and stern man. I really don't ever recall seeing him without a tie on, even for breakfast. When he came out of his room in the morning, he was fully dressed and ready to go. He was always about his business. By the time Abner came along, he was a pro at raising kids.

It is a well-known story in our family how that first tent that PapaDad so loved met with a tragic fate. Due to the fact that it was positive for black people, the local Ku Klux Klan was opposed to PapaDad's preaching. They didn't want black people assisted or encouraged. Dad told how one day, the Klan came by the service full of people and started throwing rotten eggs and tomatoes at them. The Klan members burst into the service and told PapaDad while he was preaching, "Nigger, why don't you go pick cotton?"

This makes me think of one of his quotes passed down throughout the family. PapaDad used to say, "I don't know what a scared man feels like." He told the Klan members, "I haven't planted any cotton, I don't have a sack to pick with and thank you very much, but I will go on preaching the Gospel until I die." Dad told me many times how later that night, the Klan came back and burned the tent to the ground. Although I'm sure this was devastating while living through it, for them it was actually a blessing in disguise. PapaDad then got together with some of his faithful members and they bought a house. Back then, these men may not have had a lot of formal education or jobs but they had skills. They had carpenters, plumbers, and electricians who could build anything. They knocked the walls out of the house and turned it into a church, a building much more stable and stronger than the tent which served to kick it all off.

PapaDad was a natural leader of men who has always been described to me by those who knew him best as a master at communication. Abner told a funny story about that. PapaDad traveled a lot on church business and Dad was a young boy full of energy and vigor. Dad always told me how PapaDad would ask him every time before he left on a trip, "Do you want me to whip you now or when I get back?"

As a young boy, Dad had a special friend in Denton. One of the non-relatives who lived on their street was Reverend Basinger, who liked Dad a lot. He had a mule named Kate that he rented out to people. At this time, everyone had a garden or grew food one way or another. They didn't have tractors and such, so it was common to use a mule to plow the ground which would lead to the family producing its own vegetables and fruit. Dad loved the mule; Reverend Basinger would let him feed Kate every day and Dad was the only kid allowed to ride Kate. He said he always felt special riding Kate around the neighborhood. A small thing, yes but my point is that Dad was a kid who had a rich life. Even though segregation was the rule of the day, kids didn't know it. They didn't think much about what they may not have had. In his mind, he was riding high, never missed a meal, had a lot of family surrounding him, and the spiritual training he was receiving made for a solid person.

One day, a rumor swept through the black community in Denton that the Klan was supposedly coming to southeast Denton that night to burn down the black neighborhood. This was taken very seriously as things like that had happened in other black communities. They said they were going to start with the preacher's house. They miscalculated about those Haynes and Alexander men. They were not steppin, fetchin, grinning black men of that time. Dad recalls hiding under the bed with his sister as they waited for the war to start. Fortunately, cooler heads prevailed and nothing happened that night. I mention this incident for the younger readers who would have no concept of this kind of life. This illustrates the progress we have made as a nation. Those under 60 years old have never experienced the level of hate and prejudice that existed in the 1950s.

As I interviewed Dad multiple times to lock down what he wanted to communicate to his friends and fans about his father, he would tell me how PapaDad prepared his children for the battles they would face as adults. He prepared them in many ways over the years. Obviously, PapaDad didn't know what the future held but he knew the better his children were prepared individually, the better they could help serve the Lord, the church members, the community, and themselves.

Dad knew all along that the structure, purpose and mission of the church helped him immensely. The church was a wonderful training ground for the whole family. PapaDad would bring home contracts, papers and books and always shared with his family the actual operation of the church. One of Dad's jobs was counting and rolling up the change that was given in the offerings at church. In fact, knowing him and hearing the stories from my Dad and uncles and aunts, PapaDad would insist on everyone in the house participating. At a time when blacks were lucky if anyone in a family was allowed to work and education was surely hard to come by, this black family was learning and growing by leaps and bounds. Dad would tell me that even at home, they always operated with order and purpose.

PapaDad proved to be such an effective leader that he was called upon to do more, to lead more people which led the church to promote him to Overseer for the whole state of Texas. This was the reason the family moved from Denton to Dallas. PapaDad had over 30 churches to oversee just in and around Dallas. In later years, as the church continued to grow and flourish, it divided the state into more manageable jurisdictions.

PapaDad knew and was working closely with the founder of The Church of God In Christ, Bishop Charles Mason. PapaDad was a pivotal factor in the success of Abner Haynes.

There is a family story about Bishop Mason. The founder of the entire church came to the Haynes home in Dallas. I've been told by others that people would actually faint when they passed through his shadow. An obviously anointed man of God, Bishop Mason was there to work on the church in Texas with PapaDad. Blacks couldn't stay in hotels back then, so Bishop Mason was going to stay with them at the house. It was a huge deal; at the same time young Abner had his own agenda. There was some big football game coming up that Saturday, which Dad desperately wanted to see. To you younger readers, this is the 1940's. Most people, let alone blacks, didn't have televisions in their homes yet. Dad called up the local appliance store and played like he was Bishop Haynes. He ordered a brand-new TV which the store promptly delivered. My grandmother told me this story many times as it was so very funny to her. Dad's desire to see the game got the best of him; his mother told him your father is going to kill you. Well, as it turns out, they delivered the TV just before Bishop Mason arrived at the house. Everybody was on edge because TV in the house was a new thing that black people weren't really sure about. They were all nervous about how the great man, Bishop Mason would react. All ended well however, as Bishop Mason walked in and immediately started praising PapaDad for being so forward thinking and progressive by having a TV in his home; all was forgotten about Dad buying it without permission.

Chapter 2:
Lincoln High School

One of those defining times in my Dad's life came as a result of PapaDad's success. Due to his promotion, no more would it be the small-town charm of Denton. The peace, calm and security of having family all around would be altered. Dad always felt like this move helped him mature greatly. Think of it — he was the youngest and had been playing sports with his older brothers and their friends for years. Now his mental maturity was getting a chance to catch up to his physical maturity. Just walking to school at Lincoln was going to be an eye opener. Due to the times, most black men were excluded from most everything and had nothing to do. Grown men hung out at the high school, and walking through the streets of South Dallas was sure to bring daily surprises. It was a rough area back then, populated by a lot of idle men who had little hope left in life. It's not like that now, but Dad was walking a gauntlet just to get to school every day. He had to grow up quickly.

At the time in Dallas, due to segregation, there were only two high schools black students could attend, Booker T. Washington or Lincoln. There were so many people moving to Dallas at the time that the junior high schools, which blacks could attend, were all overcrowded. The day the family went to enroll Abner for the eighth grade, they were informed that the entire eighth grade class would be going on to the high schools. My Dad was a part of the only class at Lincoln High School that went there for five years because there was no room for them at the junior high as eighth graders.

He played football at Lincoln with kids much older than him. I've always thought this had something to do with the athlete that he eventually became. They played pickup games every day at lunch time. Dad told how they played a game called "Pitch It Up". There might be 50 boys out on the field; they would throw the ball up in the air and whoever caught it tried to score. It would be the guy with the ball against everyone else. Excellent training ground for broken field running! Dad's football experience with his older brothers back in Denton served him well.

Abner had always felt a special bond with Lincoln High School and the men and women who operated it. These were black educators who were keenly aware of what blacks faced in the 1950s and they were going to do their part to have the kids ready for the world they would have to succeed in. After the first several weeks of school, playing their game at lunch, the head track coach, Brad Brashear noticed Dad and told him, "You can be my hurdler". Dad told me he didn't even know what a hurdler was but he felt like if the coach thought he could be one, that was fine by him.

My Dad's first big sporting success came through track & field. He didn't even play football as a freshman but he ran track. As a sophomore, Dad won the state championship in the hurdles. He was a sprinter and hurdler. He really loved track. I remember him telling me more than once how after he won that state championship as a sophomore, people started to notice him. People patted him on the back. He saw that they had a certain pride in the school and the community because he had won. Those who had always brushed him off or ignored him before, now wanted to talk with him. People in the neighborhood started to know his name; it was a tremendous accomplishment and vaulted his sports career to the forefront.

Dad always had a great deal of respect for Coach Brashear. He would tell me throughout the years, stories of how the coach would pile six or seven of them in his car and off they went to Houston, Austin, Galveston or wherever. Six or seven runners were all they needed. That gave the coach a 440 relay and mile relay team. All the runners would compete in individual events like the 100, 200, high jump and all the other events at a track meet. Dad told how they would go into meets and win the whole thing with five guys. Coach Brashear was a great coach who understood young men. Instead of dodging, he had his boys running against stiff competition. They ran against the top black schools in Texas. Jack Yates and Wheatley of Houston, Jefferson Moore of Waco, I.M. Terrell of Ft. Worth, Austin Anderson and others. The boys gained confidence from running against these top programs. Dad loved track which made putting in the hard work necessary to excel in track & field doable. They all worked at it and continued to refine and polish the God given talent they had. Coach Brashear knew to make sure they had the experience of facing these legendary programs and it all worked out. In time they knew that they had won in Houston, San Antonio and Ft. Worth so that meant they could win anywhere.

Coach Brashear was a very well-respected coach in Dallas. He was friends with several of the coaches at the white schools. Those white coaches — through sport — were probably farther along than the general public regarding race. They knew it was best for their runners to run against good competition as well. They didn't care what color the competition was. So, coach Brashear had the Lincoln track team practice with the all-white team from Sunset High School in Dallas. My Dad would always tell me of this great runner they had. Eddie Southern ran the quarter mile. He would go on to run for the University of Texas and won a silver medal at the 1956 Olympics. They couldn't compete against each other officially as we couldn't have blacks running with whites in the 1950s but they did it anyway and both sides were better athletes because of it.

It was not only sports for Dad; the church belonged to the whole family and everyone was expected to pitch in and help. The Haynes kids knew the members and their children would be watching them to see how they handled themselves and that knowledge helped them all to behave and develop in a positive manner. Being the pastor's kid really helped Dad in untold ways. He had structure and purpose when others fell by the wayside. He was with it. He didn't rebel against his father or the church. It was his identity and his world long before sports ever came up. He often told me how some friend of his may have suggested doing something not right, but my Dad couldn't go along because he had to go to choir practice or some other church activity. Who knows what that may have saved him from?

This was the atmosphere Abner grew up in. His family was already leading other black people when he came along. From the beginning, they were being taught and developed into solid human beings just through the everyday workings and solving of problems that go along with the churches and their members individually. A very solid foundation for any kid to get started. We still have relationships today that started through the church.

Dad told a funny story about how the football part of his life started at Lincoln. He started playing football as a sophomore. There were so many kids and good athletes that everybody pretty much treated him like just another guy. His sophomore year however was different. They started him out at linebacker. Lincoln had a great senior running back named Elijah Walker. On one particular play, Dad met Elijah in the hole; after they unraveled the pile, Walker was bleeding and unconscious. The head coach Farley Lewis told Dad, "You knocked him out, you get in there and play his position." Dad never gave up the job after that. This was the beginning of his football career.

Chapter 3:
1956

It was 1956, Abner was a multiple state champion in high school who wanted to continue on to college. He certainly could go to Prairie View A&M University, as two brothers and a sister already attended. All of the black schools were recruiting Dad. He could have gone to Grambling, Texas Southern, Florida A&M or a host of others.

At this time in Texas and the south in general, neither the school districts nor university systems were integrated. It was separate and unequal, of course. My Dad told me many times about this time in his life. How they received hand me down, used textbooks from the white schools. Many times, the books they had to use were filled with scrawled racist messages, recorded by the white students who got the books when they were new. The sports equipment they used was also second rate. The track team had one hurdle for Dad to practice with until coach Brashear had the workshop at the school make a few more. It was very tempting for Dad to leave the state and the south as the University of Colorado and others were recruiting Dad heavily, encouraging him to remove himself from the oppression of the south by coming to their schools which were not segregated.

We had relatives who lived in Denver and my Dad had already been there as a kid, spending the first grade there. Even then, Colorado was not segregated. They didn't have the deck artificially stacked against everyone who was not white, so I think they were the leaders in his mind.

Dad told me many times, of being raised in segregated Jim Crow Texas all his life only to finally get to experience the joy of integration, no longer being singled out for mistreatment because of the color of one's skin. No more separate but unequal. He'd speak of how refreshing it was just to go about a normal day in Colorado. That even the elementary schools were integrated. They really wanted him; everyone wants to feel wanted, and according to Dad he was very tempted and could have easily ended up at the University of Colorado. Integration in the south may have been delayed by years, and there are thousands that benefited from it that would not have had the chance.

Recruiting was different back in those days. Colorado sent a guy named Willie Walls to recruit Dad. He wanted him so badly that he drove a pink Cadillac right up to the front of Lincoln. Dad remembered this day vividly as it caused quite a stir and commotion in South Dallas first, then at Lincoln. Recruiting wasn't done like that back then. Normally white universities didn't send anyone into a black area like South Dallas to do anything.

The way Dad explained it to me over the years, it was the Bishop, his father, who started to mention that Dad was a good football player and he was going to be all right wherever he went to college, but he could do something that helped everybody, black and white.

It was always Dad's final decision to make but the family was well known in Denton where UNT was located and that had a great appeal to him as well as Colorado.

Texas or anywhere else in the south did not allow blacks to play football at their universities. It was not how it is today back then. PapaDad had seen and knew all too well what the members of his church went through in their daily lives. Their children were probably not great athletes, like Abner, that universities would seek to add to their teams. The Bishop thought that if his son, my Dad, could successfully integrate and go to school with whites, they would start to understand that we were capable of doing so without harm to white students. Abner could help to break down some of the stereotyping of that time — that we couldn't be on time, we weren't trustworthy, we couldn't do the coursework etc. He would tell Dad that he would be challenged and would run into prejudice and hate at a white school in Texas, but if he met the challenge and overcame the obstacles, it could have long lasting implications. He explained to Dad how his decision on where he would go to college could help the church members' children be able to attend a university themselves.

They were developing the vision of breaking down a gigantic barrier that held our people back. PapaDad thought that other kids would see what Abner was doing and get inspiration for their own dreams. On top of all the good that could potentially be done, Dad knew he had several aces in the hole so to speak in Denton that would help make the daunting task more doable. Dad knew he had relatives nearby and that PapaDad had real friends and respect in Denton, white and black, which would make things smoother. In time, after much deliberation, Dad settled on accepting the challenge of integration at North Texas State in Denton, Texas. Although there were many challenges still ahead, his path was set.

Chapter 4: Integration

Dad often remarked to me how they didn't have to call the National Guard to escort him to class like in some situations. While there were certainly people against integration, the people of Denton didn't riot in the streets at the thought of blacks and whites playing football together. Dad thought the people of Denton, as well as the University of North Texas, should be commended and recognized for what they did. They were the first in the south to do this with a black athlete. The vision and leadership they showed positively affected so many students who came after Dad. It was nine years later when SMU in Dallas accepted their first black player, Jerry LeVias. It was 15 years later when the University of Texas in Austin welcomed their first black player. So you see, although not everyone approved, the people of Denton and key individuals at UNT were forward thinking and more fair minded than what was happening everywhere else in the south which was a blessing for all who were involved.

My father and I talked for years as he would tell me of his upbringing and football career. Sure, he had God given talent, but to negotiate being the first to break down such a volatile and emotional barrier as segregation took a special person as well as special circumstances. Yes, Dad could have gone to integrated Colorado but he also had a chance to change the system in Texas and the south for untold others who would now have opportunity at higher education instead of being artificially excluded. I think that is what PapaDad knew would happen. He knew his own son and he knew the people of Denton. PapaDad was sure Abner Haynes could do it.

Dad felt like his story was not that of the evil or racist white people. That's not what he would highlight. Although I speak the truth about what happened, that's not the focus of this book. We don't seek to place blame. It is the story of those who were further along in their thinking. It is the story of people who were fair enough to at least give him the chance to compete. It is the story of young men coming together in defense of what was right. An American story of overcoming adversity, hard work, perseverance and courage. Dad expected opposition, he never gave much thought to those who were against him; just like today, many times the haters were the loudest in putting forth the day's bigotry. He wanted to make sure his fans know of those who made a difference, those who were on his side and supported him. Those who were about fairness and equality. They were exactly the right group of people at the right time in history. While at other schools, they were busy explaining how blacks couldn't do this or couldn't do that, these individuals at UNT stepped out in faith which upended the status quo.

There were specific people who were difference makers in this process of going first with integration in the south that I know my father would like you to know about. One of PapaDad's great friends was W.C. Orr. He was the president of the biggest bank in Denton. A man I myself met as I came through UNT.

J.C. Matthews was the president of the university. My Dad told me through the years of how Dr. Matthews would be sitting in the bleachers, watching practice almost every other day. He wanted to ensure that Abner got a fair shake. Head coach Odus Mitchell was a fair man who Dad said always treated him with respect. At one point, Coach Mitchell instructed the white players who were still against Dad to not refer to him in any kind of ethnic way. He told them, "If you can't call him by his name, don't call him at all."

Fred McCain was one of my Dad's coaches. He along with his wife Mary were very kind to Dad. I knew them both; they looked out for Dad. They were solidly in his corner at all times and helped Dad navigate this new world he found himself in. Coach McCain was from Gainesville Texas, which had a sizable black population. He told me before he passed away that he had black friends there in Gainesville since he was a boy. Knowing blacks was not new for him, and he didn't automatically hate them like others of his day. Zeke Martin was another of PapaDad's friends. He owned a restaurant in Denton. He and Dad became great friends as Mr. Martin told Dad, "You'll never go hungry here. If you need to eat, come here." I knew Mr. Martin as well and he made some of the best hamburgers in Texas.

There are too many people to list who helped or made positive contributions. It was truly a community effort. Dad wanted to make sure people understand that it's not just his story. His teammates got over their own personal misgivings as they jelled and became a cohesive unit. The leadership at UNT showed tremendous courage and vision when others perpetuated exclusion and hate. While there was opposition to integration, the people of Denton didn't rebel or create problems that so many other places endured during this difficult time in history. It was a perfect synergy of good, fair-minded people and a great athlete. Preparation was meeting opportunity. This is what it took to break down the color barrier in Texas and the south and that's exactly what they did.

Mr. Martin, for example, knew he may have to be called on. Although the school was going to allow Dad to try to make their team, there were many practical areas that had not been addressed yet. When my Dad started his college career, blacks could not eat on the school's campus and they certainly could not sleep there. I believe there was actually a law against it in Texas; it simply wasn't done. After each two a day practice, Dad would have to walk or hitch hike back to the black part of town to eat and get some rest in the scorching August heat of Texas after the morning practice, while his teammates easily did these basic things a couple blocks away right there on campus. Then he would have to walk back across town for the afternoon practice. This further makes the point of the difficulty he faced and overcame.

Dad could see the deck was stacked against him. He could see his teammates didn't have to walk across town after practice. It was unfair of course but the thing is, Dad was not looking for fairness. Our family already knew the system in 1956 was not fair before he went there. He had set his mind on his goal and with the help of his father was able to ignore and block out the noise of bigotry. Let's face it — they were already experts at life not being fair. Abner's mother and father had prepared him for this kind of situation. They had Dad believing he was on that campus for a specific purpose and that the challenges were just a test of his faith and character. Some people don't understand the impact of the church here. PapaDad was very well respected at this time; he was overseeing many churches in Texas. Black people all over Texas knew about Abner and his effort to integrate. They felt a part of his effort to get white people to understand we were not the enemy. They felt hope and optimism for their own children's prospects in life because of what Abner was doing. Black Texas was solidly behind him and knew his fate would affect their own as well as their children's fate. What if he went to North Texas and robbed something? What if he couldn't be coached? What if he couldn't be trusted? The stereotypes of the day would have been reinforced; the bigotry would be upheld. The haters would have won, and thousands who received education probably wouldn't have even been allowed to try. North Texas would have been like other schools that waited another 15 years to try to assimilate blacks into their campus culture. They would be able to say we tried but blacks can't integrate with us. Dad knew all this the day he arrived. I believe it was a tremendous weight for him to bear on

18-year-old shoulders but on the other hand, I know that helped him to watch his own behavior, to rein in his own tongue. It probably helped him to take more than a young man might take without the gravity of all these others' dreams hanging in the balance.

Although he couldn't eat on the campus, Dad had an Aunt Essie there in Denton. One of those aces in the hole, Aunt Essie owned a cafe in the black part of town. PapaDad was secretly giving her money each month to ensure Abner could eat there. Dad also had a sister and her husband living in Denton. Even though the university at that point didn't care where or if he ate anything, the fact of the Haynes family's position in Denton gave my Dad options that another black player with roots in Houston or San Antonio would not have had. Again, the perfect person to demolish the separation and overcome the other stumbling blocks to integration that would be presented. You can see that Abner was not an outsider trying this thing. He and his family were local people and I think that had a great deal to do with the roaring success they all enjoyed.

Chapter 5:
First Practice

We have discussed for years that first day of practice Dad's freshman year. I've never seen him so animated, however, as one particular night when we went through the whole thing. He had mentioned it before, of course, but this night I was about 20 years old and Dad knew I now understood a lot more about the world. He had recently purchased the land that would later become the Circle H Ranch. We didn't have any houses or buildings on it this night, but we used to have a lot of fun together out on the land all kind of different ways. We just both enjoyed nature and experiencing life out of the big cities as well. I had come up with an idea and Dad was with it. We bought a large tent in Dallas, which I spent half that day erecting out on our land in a nice clearing that was surrounded by towering 200-foot pine trees. We caught a few fish, cleaned them and cooked them right there in front of our tent. They had been alive an hour earlier and we really value fresh food. In this kind of relaxing setting, I knew Dad was feeling good and he usually had such interesting stories to tell that I was anticipating what we would talk about as the sun was setting. We roasted a pot of coffee up over the open fire we had going just like in the old western movies and enjoyed the stars and clean air as Dad started to tell me what he remembered about that first day at UNT.

He and his high school teammate Leon King arrived at the stadium in a cab. He could see much of the team gathered and milling around. Up until that time, Dad came from the segregated black world. He had never played football with a white person, nor ever had a white friend. He was, however, coming from Lincoln High School and South Dallas, so he was not intimidated. He thought of his own father, knowing PapaDad would not entertain fear; they were taught to overcome fear, not be paralyzed by it. He told me that he immediately noticed three of the players heading his way. Dad — I think — initially thought they were the enforcers who were coming to let him know he was not welcome.

An interesting fact in all of this is that the school had not informed the white players that the team was going to be integrated now. The way I understand it, they found that out on the same first day of practice. Coach Ken Bahnsen told me on multiple occasions that Head Coach Odus Mitchell didn't even inform all of his assistant coaches beforehand, let alone the players. That first day of Dad's freshman year turns out to be quite the inflection point that keeps coming up. Some white players quit the team immediately, while others refused to use the showers because of the black teammate. Remember, the white players came from all-white worlds. Most came from small towns that didn't have a single black person in the whole school district. You can imagine what they were taught and believed about blacks at the time — so they too had a massive hurdle to overcome without advance warning. The three players who made the first move to speak to my Dad were not enforcers at all. They were a credit to the family that raised them; they showed what they had been taught at home and where they were coming from. They were just three guys with good hearts who didn't have an ounce of prejudice in them. It was Vernon Cole, the quarterback, his older brother Charlie, and Garland Warren. They told my Dad, "Welcome to North Texas." It was on.

The times were different; the team was different from a typical college football team of today. One of the three who came out to welcome Dad and the first to extend his hand was Charlie Cole. Dad told me that Charlie was 24 years old then. A grown man who had already fought in the Korean war. Charlie explained to Dad in later years that he had already been in the integrated Air Force for four years. He had already had the experience of working side by side with black men in the military. He told Dad they ate together in the same mess hall and they slept together in the same barracks. He had finished his Air Force tour and was back to play football and finish his education. Charlie exuded positive leadership and maturity; he was one of the many difference makers for the team. Think of his point of view as opposed to the 18-year-old who had never been around black people and simply carried on with the prejudices he had been taught. Those three were amongst the leaders who allowed this great experiment to work.

Charlie's younger brother was Vernon Cole, the quarterback. Vernon was a great friend. Dad told me so much about him, I feel like I knew him. They were from Pilot Point, Texas. Vernon had grown up on a farm and like Dad, who had never had a white friend, Vernon had never had a friend who was black. For whatever reason, they immediately hit it off. They just had a certain chemistry with each other. Vernon was a very good athlete who could run, throw, and was fearless. He always showed confidence and leadership. Dad often told me how, in the beginning, whites risked being ostracized on campus for speaking or dealing with him, but that Vernon Cole didn't care. All students on campus were not for the integration of the university, just like all football players did not agree. After practicing in the sweltering August heat of Texas Dad would start his long walk back to the black part of town to rest and eat. As soon as he got going there was Vernon Cole. He would walk part of the way with Dad in solidarity. He was a great person and friend. As Dad could not eat on the campus in the beginning, it was Vernon who would go into the cafeteria and sneak food out to my Dad to keep him from going all the way back across town before having something to eat.

Of course everyone was not as supportive of Dad's efforts. There was another point of view that Dad had to contend with. He would tell me of his conversations with his teammates that they had years later after passions had cooled and integration was the norm. These guys were teammates who had battled an overcome together and could talk honestly to each other.

Some of the things his teammates have told him over the years regarding the white players' initial reaction to the new reality that was thrust upon them in 1956. According to them, receiver

Mac Reynolds was reported to have said, "Man, I don't like this. I don't want no niggers on the team. This is our school and our team. They got their own schools. Why don't they go play with their own kind?"

Later on that first day after the coaches arrived, they moved on to getting their equipment and lockers. Dad was unloading his equipment in his locker when he noticed the guy next to him, Gordon Salsman gathering all of his stuff up. He moved down to the other end of the locker room accompanied by the laughter of some of the white players. He moved next to another of the running backs, John Darby from Pampa Texas. He asked Salsman what he was doing and Salsman replied, "I don't want to be over there next to HIM."

Darby asked again to make sure everyone heard, "So you're not going to use that locker?"

When Salsman replied no, then Darby told everyone, "Then I am." Darby was from Pampa Texas, where my Dad's brother was a young preacher. Dad had even been to Pampa to visit his brother and after this showing by Darby, they became fast friends. Dad really appreciated the gesture but it remained true that not all the players were on board with integration of the team.

The team somehow got through that first day. As I stated earlier some quit, some refused to shower because of the black person, others stayed but didn't associate with Dad; each slowly dealt with their individual concerns as they turned their attention to winning football games as the season was rapidly approaching.

The more they dealt with one another, the more of a team they became.

Again, Dad had talked for years with these same men, the ones who will speak honestly about those days. Some have related to him that they initially wanted Dad to be run off. They were the ones in the dominant position, so they didn't care anything about fairness or what was right and wrong. They were slapped in the face with progress on that fateful first day of practice at North Texas. They had lived their entire lives in the all-white world and they weren't ready to change that. They did not think the mixing of races on their football team was a good thing. They wanted things to remain as they always had been. Of course, this makes sense because that's just the way it was with the general public. That was the thought and law of that time. They probably thought that no food, walking across town to sleep and eat and all the other negativity would cause Dad to quit. In fact, while many felt like this, there were others who felt differently. Dad always told me of those who supported him and most of these men I have known myself. Frank Cline and Jim Shurburn were two who come to mind. They are both great friends of Dad's to this day. Vernon Cole, Raymond Clement and Duane Day were further along in their thinking. Coaches Fred McCain, Herb Ferrill and Ken Bahnsen were experienced leaders who played key roles in victory for all. Charlie Cole, Joe Mack Pryor, Robert Duty, George Herring, G.A. Moore, Bruce Simmons, Bill Carrico, Dan Smith, Don Smith, Frank Lawless, Sammy Stanger, Terry Parks, Noe Flores, Chao Sandivol, Jerrel Shaw, Bobby Way, Joe Oliver were all Dad's teammates who became lifelong friends. I'm sure I'm not listing everyone and I apologize, but they know they were there. They walked through the fire of life together and came out as better men. This group of young men paved the way of race integration for so many to follow. There is another that I must mention, as we camped out that night Dad told me really for the first time about Norman Miller. Mr. Miller wasn't a player on the team. He was one of the male cheerleaders. Mr. Miller was a dedicated and fearless friend to my Dad. He would openly walk and talk to Dad on campus and he didn't care who knew it or didn't like it. At that young age he was already an outstanding person. I can tell by the expression on his face that Dad really appreciated him. Mr. Miller later in life went on to be the Founder and CEO of Interstate Battery Corp.

They are, "The Bald Eagles," an organization the North Texas players from that freshman team formed after their careers, to celebrate the accomplishments of the team and remain connected with each other. I have been honored to attend many of these meetings of the Bald Eagles with Dad. I was his driver from a young age and I loved football so it was just natural. We'd have a great day as the families had an opportunity to meet, relax together, share a meal, tell stories and keep up with each other. We'd meet at different locations and cities. One of Dad's greatest friends from that team was Raymond Clement from Bowie, Texas. When the Bald Eagles started, Raymond's granddaughter Emma, was three. She is a grown woman now and Dad was her God-Father. Our families remain joined at the hip to this day.

Raymond related to us many times some of the issues and facts that Dad couldn't have known at the time. He was able to fill in many blanks about what the white players went through and what they really thought before they had time to know Dad as a person. Raymond had only attended segregated schools; in fact, he told us that Bowie didn't have any blacks in the whole town. According to Raymond, he had never played with a black or against a team with a black player on it. He went on to tell Dad, he had never even had a conversation with a black person until he met Dad. Raymond made significant changes in his own attitudes as he got to know Dad. He was a great man and friend who is truly missed.

Bill Carrico was another of the young men who turned out to be a great friend, a man of honor. Mr. Carrico was an outstanding offensive lineman. He started his career at the University of Texas and then transferred to North Texas. He would get very agitated as the teams' opponents would try to intimidate my Dad with racial slurs and insults. Dad told me of one particular game where the insults were flying freely. Mr. Carrico told the opposing defensive lineman, "Don't call him that anymore." The defensive lineman replied that he didn't say it, so Bill picked him up and body slammed him to the turf and told him, "Well, you tell whoever did say it, to not say it anymore". From that point on in that game, they just played without the racial barbs. These men got to know Dad, stood up for him, protected him and I'd dare to say that they all loved each other as teammates who went through some harrowing things together, which eventually made this world a better place.

It was Coach Fred McCain that told me this story. In Dad's first year, the rules were that freshmen could not play on the varsity, however good they were. The coaches had set up a scrimmage between the varsity and the freshman team as they prepared the varsity for their opening game against Ole Miss. The scrimmage drew a big crowd as UNT fans were eager to get a look at the team. The players took this scrimmage very seriously as the varsity was not going to be shown up by a freshman team. Particularly a freshman team with a black on it. Dad started at running back and on the game's first play, Coach McCain told me he remembers hearing one of the varsity players yelling, "Watch that coon, watch that coon!"

Quarterback Vernon Cole made a simple handoff to Dad. He started right but there were three or four defenders waiting for him. He then reversed field and weaved through the varsity defense for an 80-yard touchdown run. Dad's freshman teammates went wild, they all ran the length of the field to congratulate him, as they were I think surprised that they could compete with the varsity players. At that moment, there was no black and white. They were just a team; yes, a freshman team, but a team nonetheless. They celebrated and bonded, which would be what sustained them with all they would still have to face. Coach told me that run did multiple things for all involved. For the varsity team, it instantly demolished the myth that black players weren't good enough to compete with whites. With that single run, Dad gained a measure of respect and began to be accepted by his teammates as they could plainly see that Abner could help them win.

Dad always told me that it was the late Herb Ferril, one of the varsity coaches, who told him later, "That was the last time we heard anything about coons".

It's a little ironic but Dad was surely more prepared for what awaited them as a team with a black player in an all-white world. Dad knew about unfairness, racism and bigotry just from living in the USA as a black person. You probably could say it was normal and for us, unfortunately, a part of everyday life. While it took some teammates longer than others to get their mind wrapped around the concept of playing football with a black person, they all were confronted squarely in the face with the hate that was normal in that time. This was Texas in 1956. Passions over the issues of race run deep, even today. The incidents and threats were being made in a state that can be violent, by people willing to act. Think about it — all of Dad's teammates came from all-white towns, all-white schools and all-white football programs. They had always been accepted and celebrated by their peers; that's all they knew. As a white person, they had never experienced being the subject of hate or bigotry. That was for blacks. They wouldn't have realized it that first day at practice of course, but they were about to see and learn first-hand the insults, indignities and inherent unfairness that was the rule of the day for black people.

It wasn't only in Texas; when the team went on the road to play other all-white teams, it would seem that all the white guys on the UNT team were guilty of something to hate them for. The opposing team's fans were not just against the black guy. The rest of the UNT team and coaches were guilty as well for being with or bringing the black guy. This was new for them, being the object of hate. I've had Dad's teammates admit to me after seeing for themselves the kinds of things that were said and done to Dad — they were ashamed of their own people. Maybe they began to see for themselves, a little, the position of a black person in 1956. Dad would tell me that at times, even he was surprised by the level of the vitriol. The incidents they all went through toughened them up however and produced an undefeated freshman team. In time, it brought the team, school and city of Denton closer together. In time, the UNT side, players, coaches, administration and fans got tired of the way they were all being treated simply because they decided to give a young man a chance. After going through the blood, sweat and tears of two a day practices in that August heat, Abner began to be a person to his teammates. They got to know each other; many had already decided that he was a good guy. Some even thought of him as a friend. They slowly started becoming a team that looked out for one another and those fledgling relationships that started back in 1956, still flourish today.

I think all involved could see the unfairness of what Dad had to go through. He couldn't eat on the campus, could not sleep there. They heard all the death threats, name calling and vulgarity. The entire team was denied service, harassed and cursed right along with the black guy. This was all true and yet all the individuals involved rose to the occasion. Guys evolved, matured and grew. All of them, Dad included, adjusted certain attitudes for the common good. They worked through a very difficult time in our country's history and did it together. The coming together and success of the football team allowed the leadership of the school to begin cultivating and expanding the opportunity for education of minority students that didn't have anything to do with sports to what it is today.

These are but some of the thoughts and facts that Dad shared with me as we camped out on our new land. This was history being made and I am honored that I had the opportunity to know many of these men who made this experiment work, for the good of all people.

My Dad used to tell me that in certain ways, he felt like Jonah, in the belly of the whale. The fact is after working hard together, after fighting and clawing to get better, young men start to come together to accomplish the common goal. By the time they got to that season's games, Dad had a reliable crew of teammates who recognized the way he was being treated and didn't agree with it. He had friends who looked out for him. If Dad couldn't eat, no one would eat. They were a team who would stick together as they were being tested.

Chapter 6:
Corsicana Texas

The freshman team's second game was a pivotal moment in the history of the university that has been documented and is well known amongst many individuals. Here again I'm not speaking so much to you who already know the story. I know from my own generation that many are not aware of it, in fact were not even born when this happened. I tell the story to you guys. It's my attempt to ensure that the history is not lost. That those who stood for what was right are celebrated and recognized for what they did.

The team had already won their first game against Hardin-Simmons in Abilene. Everywhere they played that season created a circus atmosphere and this was no exception. They were traveling to Corsicana, Texas to play all white Navarro College. For UNT, they would have more to overcome than just the opposite team on the field. It started with the pre-game meal.

You have to understand that this was 1956; people didn't have the entertainment options that we have now, most probably didn't even have television. This game on a Saturday evening was like an NFL game for the people of Corsicana. Navarro was their team and the stadium was packed. Life and laws were different back then; nobody was monitoring anything at the stadium. It's Texas, people have guns, they are drinking, and by kickoff time they are extremely hostile to the opposing team. I'm sure that was just part of the entertainment for the night to them. They would have been against any team and for their team. By game time, the crowd was liquored up and out for blood.

Now, when I speak of knowing Dad's teammates over the years, here is an example. One of the players for UNT was a defensive end named Edgar Gray. Mr. Gray was a tall man, about 6 '6 who was from Corsicana where the game with Navarro was being played. He is a very nice man and told me of those days himself. We met and he got the chance to tell me what he remembered about this game while we were all at the University of North Texas for a football game that marked the opening of UNT's new DATCU Stadium. Mr. Gray had gone to high school there in Corsicana with many of the Navarro players. He was a junior when Dad was a freshman so he wasn't on this team; he was on the UNT varsity. For whatever reason, Mr. Gray had been home that week and told me he met with many of the Navarro players who had heard rumors that UNT had a black player. They told Edgar, "If they bring that nigger here, we will kill him." They went on to imply that at the very least, they would hurt Dad.

Edgar said he told them in response, "Y'all won't even be able to get a good lick on Abner." "You guys won't be able to hurt him; you have never played against anyone as quick as Abner."

Coach Ken Bahnsen told me about this day as well at one of the Bald Eagle meetings, which was held at his home. We had a great time that day. Coach Bahnsen had a Bar B Que and most of the members of the group were still alive that day. We sat together at one point out on his back porch sipping iced tea as he relived the day. Coach Bahnsen's pained expression showed me his distaste for what he was about to tell me. He relaxed and started explaining to me how as soon as they got off the bus at the stadium in Corsicana, four men approached him. They asked him point blank, "Are you going to play those two niggers?" Coach Bahnsen said he told them, "Yes, I intend to play all of my players." They responded with, "Then they will die tonight."

When thinking of what he would have to endure before coming to UNT, Dad wanted to have a friend with him. He and high school teammate Leon King had agreed to try to play college ball together. So there were two black players on the team.

We have all discussed for years at our Bald Eagle gatherings that this game marked the key point in the team coming together. Even in a larger sense, it was a crucial moment for the entire country playing out in this sleepy town in Texas. These 18-year-old freshmen couldn't have known the gravity of what that night meant for integration, fairness and equality. The reactions and stands that individuals took were real, not fake or an acting job. They were confronted, they were challenged, they didn't know ahead of time that they would face this kind of treatment. That means the reactions from the UNT freshman team were real. These men were warriors who hung together when bigotry and hate was all around them.

It started with the pre-game meal. A normal football ritual all the way down to little league. The team had found a restaurant there in Corsicana called The White House and Dad said the people who worked there were friendly enough, but before they all started eating, the waitress looked him straight in the eye and told him she had a place out back for Dad to eat. This was typical of the south in the 1950s. Nobody thought a thing about separating the black player from his team to eat out back like an animal. Dad always would tell me that this wasn't new or unexpected. He simply was not going to eat at all, but he was not going out back.

Everything changed in an instance however. Joe Mack Pryor who was from Fort Worth and was a mountain of a man was the first one who spoke up. He was joined by George Herring. Dad didn't have to say a word. Instead of simply enjoying his pre-game meal, siding with the day's racism, Mr. Pryor told the staff of the restaurant if Abner couldn't eat with the rest of the team, then none of them would eat either. Vernon Cole, the quarterback who was the team's leader stood up and pushed his plate away. This is the kind of character the Bald Eagles had even as young men. Instead of the nice restaurant meal they had baloney sandwiches all together as a team. This is why it is so important to know who these young men were. The stand that these white players at UNT took in defense of my Dad changed the country for the better. They just came to UNT to play football. They didn't think of themselves as trailblazers. They were just committed to what was right. Dad was so proud of his teammates for making that stand. For a bunch of guys who'd only been practicing together for four or five weeks, it was a tremendous show of support and solidarity. This is why they all love each other, and to think they were just 18-year-old freshmen at that time. Variations of this same story would continue to rear its head for them in the future in Kentucky, California, Oklahoma, Utah, and others.

Dad told me there was a little rickety fence separating the field from the stands so the UNT freshman team had to walk right past the crowd to get to the field.

The liquored-up crowd went ballistic at the sight of a black player in uniform; not only did UNT have nerve enough to send a black player, there were two of them. It just wasn't done in 1956. Blacks playing football with whites — what would be next! Dad recalls the Navarro fans stomping and shouting; to him it seemed like the stands were shaking. I've had Dad's teammates describe this to me as well. They spoke of the fans seemingly foaming at the mouth and purely out for blood. The racial slurs and references were hurled at them non-stop; it was truly a mob mentality.

Many of the Bald Eagles have told me that there were a few gunshots that went off. Most of the hate was directed at the blacks of course, but Dad's white teammates started to learn what they were in for, as well. They were called "nigger lovers" and all kinds of other things. According to the Bald Eagles, this was a first for them. They had never felt disrespect and hate directed at them. As a team, they were stunned as the game started. They were 18-year-old kids just trying to play a game.

They were not prepared for the level of venom that was hurled at them.

As the team came out for the game and walked to the field along the little fence that any five-year-old could climb, the crowd started a chant, "KILL DEM NIGGERS, KILL DEM NIGGERS."

The team wasn't ready for this. They were definitely rattled. This was a night game and someone kept turning the lights off and on when UNT had the ball, which fueled the team's anxiety even more. I would imagine that the game plan wasn't the top thing on their minds. I've heard this incident described by so many who were there. They all remember different aspects of this game. One thing that was unanimous is they all realized this was the point in history where they came together as a team. These men would have four years to work together and things would get better, but this was ground zero for the positive changes that would come which benefited so many who came after them.

Dad's teammates changed the way they huddled up before each play. Since they had heard gunshots and the crowd was chanting, "KILL DEM NIGGERS," they huddled where the black players were in the middle. The Navarro fans would have to shoot a white player first like that. You can see the bonds beginning to grow and flourish between the members of that freshman team. In their minds, even though they were in trouble, they didn't leave Dad out to dry alone against the tide of bigotry that they faced. They closed ranks and stood for what was right. From that moment at the restaurant, Dad always felt a tremendous love and respect for his teammates for making that great stand with him. However, the team was clearly shaken as the game began.

Navarro shamelessly profited off of their home field advantage. They received the opening kick-off and marched straight down the field for a touchdown. On the ensuing kick-off, UNT fumbled deep in their own territory. In short order, Navarro went in for another touchdown. In the blink of an eye, they were up 14-0. This turn of events only incited the crowd more. They smelled blood as they could clearly see that their hostility had shaken these young men. Dad would tell me how he remembered some of his teammates with that dazed look in their eyes, staring into the stands seemingly not believing what they were caught up in. The crowd was having a blast in the stands as it seemed the hate and venom was working.

Ken Bahnsen was the perfect coach for this team. He had come to UNT from the San Francisco 49ers, which gave him experience with blacks that others lacked at the time. After that second touchdown, coach Bahnsen called the team over to try to calm them down. He needed to get his team's mind back on playing the game and away from the distractions. They all remember Bahnsen calling this time out and apparently it was successful. Shortly after that, Dad scored on a 40-yard run and it was 14-7.

Joe Mack Pryor and George Herring had already stood up for Dad at the restaurant but as the game turned nastier, they were willing to get down in the gutter with the Navarro players. Dad always told me how Mr. Pryor was absolutely furious, not scared. He was stomping guys in the pileups and Dad had to pull him off several times. He was yelling, "Don't call him that, don't call him that." George Herring was the same way; he was biting guys and throwing punches. This is almost hilarious unless you were there; the referees didn't throw a single flag the whole game. This was almost a war and there was not going to be any help for anyone as the referees probably felt like the majority at the game and didn't mind the black guy being hurt or assaulted.

Navarro was playing very hard for the win. They told Dad repeatedly during the game that they would not lose to a team with a black on it. You see, that was one of the notions people tried to hold onto. The idea that the segregation of the day was not hate but rather it was because black people were not good enough players to be able to play against whites. If not that, the next argument would be that black people couldn't do the coursework of a university.

Down by 7, UNT got the ball back and Dad took a handoff straight up the middle. A Navarro defender filled the hole and they met in a violent head on collision. Dad remembered being a little dazed by the impact but he popped right up as he knew not to be on the ground for long at any point in this game. The Navarro defender however was lying there unconscious, bleeding from his nose. As the UNT team was standing there watching, they could see the Navarro player's face starting to turn blue. Dad told me his teammates were then becoming nervous again as who knows what could happen now. Vernon Cole asked my Dad, "Butch, what did you do to him?" In time, the defender was taken off the field on a stretcher and the crowd then became absolutely enraged. Their anger was directed squarely at Dad of course for knocking their player out. Dad remembered the original chant was now changed to, "GET THEM NIGGERS OFF THE FIELD, GET THEM NIGGERS OFF THE FIELD."

Coach Bahnsen was a sharp guy; in the third quarter, he had his equipment man start gathering up all of their stuff. He had the bus driver start collecting all of their footballs and other gear; he even had the driver turn the bus around so that it was parked right next to the field. Coach Bahnsen told his team that as soon as the game was over, to turn and leave the field. He told them not to waste time shaking hands and not to remove their helmets. As soon as the game was over, they ran straight for the bus with their helmets on, amid a hail of curses, bricks and flying beer bottles. As the team made a bee line for the bus, the agitated crowd caught on that they were about to leave. The crowd surged toward the bus; the Bald Eagles have described this scene for me many times. The bus was pelted with all kinds of objects with several windows being broken out.

UNT had come back and won the actual game 39-21, but that was small. Dad scored 4 touchdowns in this game, but credit should go more to his teammates. They stood up for him. They protected him, they went against their own people to stand for what was right. They came together through this test and although they probably didn't realize it, that night in Corsicana, they started something that still stands today. They set the tone for many others to accept blacks at their universities without the sky falling. Many kids who have never heard of Abner Haynes owed their spot in college to what these young men successfully did starting in 1956.

Dad always said that the Navarro fans did them all a favor that night. Think about it — now Dad wouldn't have to explain to his teammates any longer what black people had to go through under the system that was in place in the 1950s. They now knew what it was like to be on the receiving end of hate and bigotry. That tends to change a person's perspective. His teammates saw first-hand how ugly and frightening it can be, to go up against the mob mentality.

Upon rolling home, riding back to the safe confines of Denton, there was a feeling of astonishment. They had gone into a very hostile environment, performed like champions and came out on top.

Dad said as they were riding home, George Herring came to where he was sitting and wanted to talk. He couldn't believe what they had just witnessed. He told Dad, "Man, I never dreamed you guys had to go through stuff like that. I didn't know y'all were catching that kind of hell." Dad always thought he saw his teammates change that day. He saw them protect him. He saw them stand up for him and they have all been brothers ever since.

To this day, that UNT freshman team is the only undefeated, untied team in school history. This team did some incredible bonding during this historic undefeated season that carried these young men, the school and the country to a better, fairer place where anyone can go as far as their ability will take them.

We discussed his life so frequently that I believe now he knew I would be able to tell his story and educate younger people who didn't see him play or never heard of him about the success they had. We travelled by car quite a bit. I would pepper him with questions and we would together knock the miles down until we reached our destination. Dad was so very appreciative of Coach Bahsen and McCain for their resiliency and fortitude. They were very special to him.

Another example of how the team grew together throughout this historic season was in Abilene, Texas. Dad had surgery to remove hemorrhoids earlier in that week. As it approached game time, Coach Bahnsen asked Dad if he could play. Dad told him that he could indeed play as he knew his team needed him to win. The only problem would be the fact that he couldn't sit down. How would he ride the bus from Denton to Abilene?

Coach Bahnsen came up with a solution to that. He had the players make a pallet out of the luggage rack above the seats. They laid out blankets and made Dad a nice comfortable spot to lie down on. He rode all the way to Abilene in the luggage rack. He knew his team needed him in order to win. This trip showed his teammates how tough he was. They knew then that Abner endured this pain because he was a team guy. The team's bonding and love for each other just continued to grow as they walked through these various adversities together.

Dad always had fond memories of Abilene; he used to tell me how they never had the kind of racial problems in Abilene that they had in other cities and towns. The team played there twice that year and never had any issue with eating at restaurants. Dad relates that he noticed nobody had brought up about him eating out back or in the kitchen while he was in Abilene. They were not refused service and all was smooth when they played there. In Houston or Dallas, people were still insane about blacks and whites eating together.

Now the fact is the coaches saw the issues the team was facing and the decision was made to just drive there, play the game and immediately drive back to Denton. So they never tried to stay in a hotel in Abilene; that issue was eliminated as Abilene is only a couple hours from Denton. Dad had wondered aloud many times what Abilene would have done if UNT wanted to spend the night with a black player on the team. However, he always did appreciate the people in Abilene, Texas who allowed him to just be an freshman, eat his pre-game meal with his teammates, play his game and go home without making sure he knew they hated him and wanted to degrade him as was common everywhere else.

Dad didn't lose his hemorrhoid stitches in this game. In fact, he scored 5 touchdowns and as we have talked and told the stories to each other, Dad's Bald Eagle brothers have told me that amazingly, the Hardin Simmons defense never even got Dad on the ground once.

Abilene may have been affected by a famous resident. Dad always told me about one of his and his brothers' favorite players. "Slingin" Sammy Baugh was the legendary quarterback of TCU and the Pittsburgh Steelers. Dad told me about Sammy since I was a young boy. Sammy played during the years the Haynes didn't have a television in the house. They listened to Sammy play on the radio.

He was at the time the head coach at Hardin Simmons. Dad told how he was warming up before their game and Sammy walked over to him and said, "Hey Abner." Dad looked around and saw Sammy's gigantic ten-gallon hat. Sammy told him, "Abner, I want you to relax and have a good game." He told Dad that he was a very good player and that if he continued to work hard, he would be a great player. They continued talking as Sammy reminded Dad not to be bothered by anything people say about him in this game or other games. Sammy knew the truth of the world they were living in. He went on to say that Dad should remain focused on what he was doing. What a great man Sammy was. Dad was floored that the head coach of the team he was about to play would take this time and work to build up his opponent. To Sammy Baugh, those words of encouragement were bigger than winning or losing one game — that's the kind of man he was. You see, this is the story of exceptional people of all races who were further along in their thinking than the masses. Leaders who pushed society forward in their own ways. This is the story of fairness, overcoming, togetherness, and love.

The Bald Eagles finished that season undefeated and untied but the challenges for Dad were just beginning. During that off season, one day, he was walking back to the black part of Denton from campus when he saw smoke high in the air. Dad became a little concerned as the smoke looked like it was coming from the general direction of their house. As he got closer, the smoke got clearer and as he crossed the last street and turned unto theirs, his worst fears were confirmed. Their house was almost burned to the ground when Dad arrived. Apparently, his nephews were playing with matches and started the fire. This was a tremendous blow to Dad. Thankfully, no one was injured but he lost every stitch of clothes he had. With enough challenges already lined up for each day, this added burden was devastating. Dad always told me about this day. My grandfather owned the house and my Dad's sister lived there as well with her kids. Dad couldn't sleep on the UNT campus but short of that, this was the perfect setup. His sister had to cook for her kids so he had that covered and it was in the same neighborhood where he had grown up. It was very comfortable for him and now it was all gone.

The church members and other blacks who weren't even in the church were all elated about Abner's chance and success in regard to integration. They knew if he could succeed, their own children might get more of a fair shake regarding their own life and education. People had given Dad all kinds of clothes and shoes. He had nice things in that house that burnt up — coats and shirts that were all of a sudden no more. He often told me how he felt like somehow black people's hopes and dreams for a better future were going up in that smoke. Even though he was just 19 years old, Dad knew his community, his people were depending on him to succeed. There was a lot riding on his shoulders and he would have to start all over again.

Chapter 7:
The Varsity Years

The fruits of Dad's integration efforts had immediately produced results. UNT welcomed two new black players his sophomore season. Dr. Matthews, the school's president, had an unwritten rule that they were to limit all teams to two blacks at most, but still this was progress. Two black players on the varsity and two on the freshman team. Dad and Leon King were on the varsity. Facing another season of August two-a-days, the walking and hitchhiking back and forth to the black part of town just to eat was getting very old. Dad went to coach McCain to ask if anything could be done.

Dr. Matthews, the school's president, agreed the situation was unfair and from then on, all four players were permitted to eat two meals a day at the athletic dorm. To them, maybe it didn't seem so monumental, but this was another step toward real equality for all students. For the first time in the history of the school, blacks were authorized to eat on the campus. Think about it — if Dad would have been a negative for the school or some kind of embarrassment or headache that first freshman season — UNT surely would not have recruited two more black players the next year. Already in the short amount of time he had been in college, Dad's infectious spirit and determination was helping him and other people who would come after him

The most memorable game of that season came in California. This was 1957; UNT was there to play San Jose State and even California was just like Texas in that Coach McCain could not find a hotel that would accept the team due to it having two black players. This is another example of how he would enlist our church to help. Through my grandfather, the Bishop, he would contact other church leaders of a particular area to fill in the gap. Together, the men would arrange a local black family to pick Dad up at the airport. He would stay and eat with this local family until game time. They would then bring him to the stadium to reunite with the team. This was the standard operating procedure as they ran into that problem quite regularly. I'm sure Dad would have preferred being with his teammates, but he's told me for years about this situation and it wasn't all bad.

Ironic, but he would be having the time of his life with the local black family that hosted him. It was unfortunate, the state of affairs that dictated black people couldn't stay in hotels but since that was normal and the rule of the day, he had fun with it. The local black family that would host him in the different cities were also facing racism and bigotry in their own lives. They were all pulling for Abner to succeed in this great experiment. Dad would tell me they treated him like a rock star at all the places he stayed while on road games. They would have great food and plenty of company for him.

This game against San Jose State was another occasion when UNT was tested and came together as a team. The previous season, the freshman team had done the same thing when faced with the hostility of the unruly crowd in Corsicana. This was different however, as this was the varsity — they were there representing the entire university.

San Jose had an excellent wide receiver named Ray North. He was an Olympic sprinter. This was something new at the time, certainly in college. A wide receiver with Olympic speed. North had already burned North Texas for a touchdown early in the game. Defenses just weren't ready for anyone with that kind of speed in the 50s. Coach Mitchell, trying to come up with some way to contain North, put Dad on defense. Dad told me this story for years — Coach Mitchell had Dad line up about 20 yards off the ball and his number one job was to not let North get behind him. Another wrinkle the coach had was he put one of the linebackers right over North on the line of scrimmage to rough him up and throw him off his route. San Jose had a couple black players just like North Texas and North was one of them. The UNT defense was roughing him up pretty well the whole game. Enough so that the other San Jose players were getting tired of the way North was being taken out of the game.

As the clock was winding down, San Jose was getting more and more desperate. They knew they were going to lose the game and seemed to want to get in a few shots of their own against the UNT players. Near the end of the game, San Jose was called for 3 unsportsmanlike conduct penalties in a row.

With three or four seconds left, San Jose called a timeout that they didn't have. The referees realized the error and started the clock back running. Time ran out on them before they could run their last play. Just like that, the game was over and San Jose was frustrated with the loss.

UNT had pulled off a hard fought 12-6 road victory and Dad told me that as soon as the final gun sounded, he saw the first fist fly. He always thought it was his friend Bobby Way who came from 20 yards away. Way made a beeline to a particular San Jose player that he had been battling the whole game and just absolutely decked him. The rest of the San Jose team saw this and with the frustration of not being able to run their last play, they snapped, and it was on.

The field just erupted; it quickly turned into a bench clearing brawl. Both teams were at midfield throwing punches and going at it. It wasn't a typical football fight of pushing and shoving. These guys had their helmets off and were throwing haymakers.

They later found out that a San Jose player had suffered a broken jaw but that was the worst injury. Dad was always amused with the local Denton newspaper's depictions of him and his exploits as they referred to him as the fleet footed Negro halfback. He always remembered the Denton Record Chronicle's headline when they got back home. They described it this way: "A unanimous two-way decision for North Texas," referring to the game and the fight.

Once again, they were confronted with a situation where everyone had to immediately decide where their loyalties were.

They fought and stood their ground together like brothers would. They defended one another again when the world tested them and truly bonded on that west coast trip – a bond that was never broken.

I can recall Dad and I being in Miami for the Super Bowl between the San Francisco 49ers and the San Diego Chargers in 1995. We had a great time in South Florida that week. Dad actually played for the Miami Dolphins during his pro career so he had lived down there and was very familiar with the area and all its different waterways. He was like a tour guide for me on this trip. We were there not only for the Super Bowl but also due to the fact that we were close to signing a couple of the players of the Miami Hurricanes college team, who were from Texas, for our Agency. We chartered a boat and all went deep sea fishing. Dad was reflective on this trip. He had played and lived in Miami, his memories and experiences were on his mind when he told me another story that I had not heard yet.

He was thinking of his friend from the NBA. You never know whose paths are crossing but another guy that was facing added difficulties due to unfairness was one of the greatest NBA basketball players of all time, Dad's wonderful friend Oscar Robertson. Basketball season was underway again and Dad had a thought. He wondered to himself what the black basketball players from other schools did when they came to play UNT. He wondered if they were separated from their teammates as was the case with him. He wondered if they were asked to eat their meals out back or in the kitchen as he had been asked to do. There certainly was no hotel they could sleep at in Denton in the late 1950's. Pondering all this, Dad decided to volunteer his house, so that the black basketball players from other schools could stay with them overnight as his way of serving his people even more. This arrangement served many but the one I want to tell you about was from the University of Cincinnati. Dad first met him when they both were sophomores. The great Oscar Robertson, the Big O. Oscar was a legendary college basketball player whose teams always came to Denton and beat up on North Texas. He went on to become an NBA superstar. The Big O would later be voted as one of the 50 greatest players in NBA history. A Hall of Famer, Oscar was an absolute magician with the ball in his hands. In reality, I didn't see him play back then of course, but Dad and I used to play basketball together when we were both younger. He knew a basketball player when he saw one. Dad told me Oscar was probably ready for the NBA straight out of high school. The first couple years, he killed North Texas singlehandedly so Dad hatched a plan during their senior season to try to help UNT's basketball team get a victory.

He looked on the schedule to see when Cincinnati would be coming to town and arranged a big party for Oscar there at his house. Dad's hope was that Oscar would get interested in one of the pretty North Texas girls and stay up a little too late. Everybody was in on it. They were going to try to keep him up as long as possible to hopefully slow him down during the next day's game. It was an exciting night with a house full of people and they all had a great time. At the next day's game, they were feeling pretty good about the scheme. North Texas was in the game, as The Big O came out sluggish and didn't score a single point in the first half. Someone however lit a fire under him at halftime. Oscar came out in the second half and absolutely took over the game. He scored almost 50 points in the second half alone and Cincinnati cruised to victory.

When the next season rolled around, Dad was firmly entrenched as the starting running back. He had worked at a steel mill in Dallas that summer and had put on about 10 pounds of lean muscle. He was much stronger than before. The fruits of integration were showing themselves as North Texas welcomed two new black players to the program. The first game was home against Texas El Paso but then they had two road games coming up. The first was to Des Moines, Iowa to play Drake University and then to Provo, Utah to play Brigham Young. Again, it was Coach Fred McCain who was charged with finding the appropriate accommodations for the team and just like in Texas, he had a difficult time securing a hotel for the team due to it having a black player. Leon King had left the team, so UNT only had one black player at this point. They were all reminded that this racial discrimination was not limited to the South. The previous season, they couldn't find a hotel in California; now it was Iowa and Utah, but once again it was the church that came to the rescue. Coach McCain turned to my grandfather, Bishop Haynes to find a suitable family in Des Moines and the team were old pros at overcoming the obstacles placed before them by now. These guys had been through a lot. They won against Drake 42-0 and returned home.

I think even the nationwide Church of God in Christ had a hard time coming up with a suitable black family in Provo Utah. They eventually found a family in Salt Lake City and Dad stayed with them while the rest of the team stayed at a hotel near the stadium. They weren't even in the same city!

Dad always talked to me about what he remembered about this game in Utah, as it amazed him to learn several things. He had never been in a decent sized city with no black people. It was also new for Dad to learn this was a place that didn't sell alcohol or cigarettes; they didn't even sell Coca Cola back then. All in all, a pretty strange place to a black guy from Dallas. Dad had a good game. He started on offense and defense. He got an interception, scored a touchdown and had a long punt return. Brigham Young played hard and there was some racial taunting but less than some other places according to Dad. North Texas won 12-6 and had a 4-1 record heading into conference play. They also had a high level of confidence and belief in one another. Remember, many of the key players on this varsity team were those same guys who stood together through that mob of a crowd in Corsicana as freshmen. They had been through things together that no one else knew about and they believed in each other. North Texas had a couple home games in a row. They beat Tulsa and then tied Cincinnati. Then came another road game against Wichita State. The same old problem reared its head. Coach McCain could not find a hotel in Kansas for the team to stay at due to the black player being with them. The last game of this season was against Louisville. This was the game that the ever-present racism took on a form that was different from what Dad considered usual. The Louisville players were not directing their racial venom at Dad but at his white teammates. They probably figured Dad was immune to it by that point and their aim seemed to be to get Dad's teammates to turn on him. The Louisville players called them nigger lovers, coon lovers and all kinds of things but his UNT teammates were not swayed. They blocked out the noise and won 21-10.

1959 was Dad's senior year. They were the defending Missouri Valley Conference Champions. They wouldn't be able to sneak up on anybody this year. That group of freshmen that went undefeated were the seniors now. The team had a lot of confidence entering the season. They were conference champions and they had all been tested for several years. They knew that they could count on one another; they knew from experience that they wouldn't wilt under pressure or the heat of the battle.

The 1959 team had three black players on it. The two new guys from the previous year, Billy Joe Christle and Arthur Perkins had been promoted to the varsity.

The second game that year was against UTEP in El Paso. I give special mention to them because we have always liked going to El Paso. Even in 1959 — when it was not allowed in California, Utah, Kansas, Kentucky or Ohio — the city of El Paso had no problem with the team having black players on it. The team was allowed to eat and sleep together in a hotel, no problem. Dad had his usual good game with 160 yards rushing including an 80-yard run. North Texas won 31-7 and they were now 2-0.

North Texas won the next home game against West Texas State 28-6, which brought them at 3-0 to the next road game. It was a big game against the Cincinnati Bearcats. Both teams had been voted in the pre-season as favorites to win the conference championship and both teams were undefeated.

Alas, the same old problem reared its head once again. No hotel in the city of Cincinnati would accept the team because it had black players. Again, Coach McCain contacted my grandfather Bishop Haynes, who had no trouble in the city of Cincinnati, as our church had many locations there, in lining up a black family to host the three black players in their home. We have spoken many times how these different host families felt. They were overjoyed to be called upon to help right this continual wrong. They already had heard of Abner Haynes and they knew what he was doing was going to help and further our whole race, so sure, they were willing to help. Dad always told me they treated the three of them like kings — these were all positive experiences for him. Not one time was it ever negative for him to stay with a local black family.

The North Texas defense played an inspired game and they won 21-6. Even the 6 points Cincinnati scored was off of a blocked punt deep in North Texas territory.

The UNT team won its next home game and stood at 5-0. They had the number 1 ranked offense in the nation and were garnering a lot of media attention.

The next game was huge. A road battle against the University of Houston.

Dad last told me about this game recently when we were at UNT. I had driven him up to the school in Denton, it was the homecoming game of the 2021 season I believe and Dad was in attendance because he was receiving the coveted Presidential Medal of Honor from the university President Dr. Neal Smatresk. Dad was going to walk out onto the field at halftime to receive the honor before the assembled crowd. I was a little worried about this arrangement, knowing his strength was not what it used to be. Whenever he appeared at an event, I was usually the one to accompany him ensuring he didn't trip over wiring or cables and to kind of be his eyes on whatever. Despite being 83 years old at the time, I could see the look of determination in Dad's eyes as he related the stories of North Texas that day. He was going to walk out on the field on his own two feet. He didn't want to use a wheelchair or anything else. He was determined to do it, and he accomplished his goal.

As we sat in the president's suite taking in the game and visiting with school officials Dad was introspective. I had heard all about this game on many occasions of course, but Dad was feeling grateful and blessed, he enjoyed reliving the moments that changed so much. He loved to remember those who helped make it possible so as we sat watching the game Dad wasn't really watching. He was back in Houston that great weekend as he related the story to me.

Coach Fred McCain had been scouring the entire city for a hotel where the team could eat and sleep together. Houston, Texas — the fourth largest city in America — as soon as a hotel found out the team had black players, they weren't interested. Can you imagine a hotel turning down all that business. The players, coaches, band, cheerleaders and fans. All would need to eat and all would need to sleep but no hotel wanted that money. It was more important to them to hold up the bigotry of the day.

King David Haynes, Abner Haynes Sr, Abner Haynes, Jr

Dad could tell the season they were having was having a positive effect on all concerned. The UNT fans and students were much more interested in the team than they had ever been before. The citizens of the city of Denton were solidly behind their team. The media took more interest as well. They all were doing a bang-up job of overcoming their opponents on the field and the obstacles and stumbling blocks off the field.

As preparations began for this epic clash, Head Coach Odus Mitchell was worried; this was a big game and he didn't want the team to be separated as it had been on so many occasions. After deciding that the efforts to find a hotel were futile, Coach McCain came up with a brilliant idea. He chartered a whole train to transport the team to Houston. It had a food car and multiple sleeper cars. The railroad had no objection to the team eating together or sleeping in close proximity. The train was set to pick them up in Denton and take the team all the way to downtown Houston's Union Station. The train would remain there overnight and bring them all back to Denton the next day.

They would eat on the train, sleep on the train, have pregame meetings and then take a bus over to the stadium. Somewhat unconventional, but at least they would all be together. Dad always told me he felt a little guilty about this. He knew that the three black players were the reason for all the controversy and unusual logistics. By this time, his teammates were like brothers to him. He didn't want them to have to jump through a bunch of hoops because of him.

Things don't always go the way you think they will, however. It was no problem to the North Texas players. I have also been told the story of this monumental weekend by Dad's teammates. Many of them had never been on a train before and they were looking forward to a different adventure. It was not a negative to them at all. I always saw Dad's face light up as he told me about the particulars of this Houston weekend. As word started getting out on the campus about the headache the city of Houston was giving UNT, the fans had enough. This was their team and they were tired of the way they were always treated just for attempting to be fair about this life by giving a black person the same opportunity as a white one.

The UNT students took issue as well; they felt like this was a snub to them as well as the football team. They all seemed to take this as a personal insult inflicted on them by the University of Houston and the city of Houston.

One of Dad's greatest friends during this time who always supported Abner on campus, in public or private was Norman Miller, who in time after college founded and was CEO of Interstate Batteries Corporation. Mr. Miller was a leader among the students. He got with some other fans that wanted to attend the game and they chartered another train to follow the football team's train. It was great, it had never before been done.

They had the trains all decorated with banners, signs and slogans. The team, coaches, students, cheerleaders, band and fans all went to Houston on trains together. Shortly after the football team's train got to Union Station in Houston, the fans and students' train pulled in. An impromptu pep rally broke out right there at the train station. Dad would always tell me that he had never felt that kind of togetherness and positivity before. Dad felt really connected to his school and community. What he was witnessing gave him strong hope that our people could have a better future. He really felt gratitude for those people at North Texas who stood with him and showed their support for him and equality.

While I tell the truth about the state of racial relations in the late 1950's we certainly are not trying to indict the whole city of Houston. In fact, Dad always told me next to Dallas it was the most comfortable place for him. Dad knew from experience he had the support of the black community there in Houston, which is sizable. He had already played football there and ran track while in high school. In fact, the state championship that Dad won in track was in the all black, Prairie View Interscholastic League, The PVIL as it was known was a legendary organization that produced to much talent to start naming names. Athletes, musicians, scholars and much more. To win a state championship in track & field in that league was a huge accomplishment. Dad had friends from Lincoln High School who attended Texas Southern University there in Houston. Again, all black people were hoping and praying for Dad to succeed, knowing his success would lift us all and bring our people forward. The black community of Houston was well aware of this game. This integration thing could be another door opening for our people that had previously been nailed shut. People could see that if Abner was successful at this integration thing maybe their son or daughter would be allowed to go to college instead of prevented from going. All were tired of bigotry and hate, the disrespect and unfairness.

Dad's Lincoln High School friend from Dallas, Deno Anthony, was in school in Houston at Texas Southern University. He came to the train station to take Dad back to Texas Southern's campus to a party they had organized for him. Deno was another man that I knew well myself. He finished school and operated his own Pharmacy in South Dallas on Malcolm X Blvd for years. Dad met the Texas Southern football players, their coaches and even the president of the school came to encourage him. It was a monumental weekend that Dad treasures to this day. They had a great time and won the game 7-6.

North Texas was 7-0, when another interesting thing happened. They had another road game, this time against the Louisville Cardinals. They won the game 39-7 to improve to 8-0 but Dad told me about the other things that went on as well. This is the weekend he ate his first bear steak. This was new to him and I imagine lots of you guys as well. I've never eaten a bear steak. He actually saw it on the menu, and remembered it was expensive. The entire team was allowed to stay together at the hotel in Louisville but there was a law on the books that prohibited them from eating together. The people who ran the hotel were clearly embarrassed by what they had to do. Dad remembered that each one spoke to him individually to let him know that they didn't think the law was right. They didn't feel it was right to separate Dad from his teammates. They continually apologized and wanted Dad to know they didn't have anything to do with it, that it was an old law that they didn't agree with.

He didn't know them and they didn't know him, but they sure didn't think it was right. They didn't realize of course that Dad had been through all this many times by then and he would stay on point, and accomplish the goal which brought him there no matter who didn't like him.

The team wasn't being fed the bear steak but since Dad had to eat alone, away from his teammates, as a way of apologizing I think, they told Dad he could have anything he wanted to eat. Dad was adventurous and in the middle of a unique experience so he ordered the most exotic thing on the menu, the bear steak. Despite the antiquated law in Kentucky these were nice, good people. There was a mixture of blacks and whites that worked at the restaurant and every one of them came to talk to Dad while he ate. They had words of encouragement and wanted to make sure Dad wasn't lonesome. I know from seeing the emotion on Dad's face as he'd tell me these things that these people at that hotel in Louisville were decent and friendly people. Yes, the archaic law was still on the books but in the end by game time, Dad was feeling pretty good; he was upbeat and ready to go.

UNT lost the next game to the University of Tulsa, which ruined the undefeated season. The game was played in Tulsa which can get very cold in the winter. At the kickoff, it was about ten degrees with a fierce north wind blowing. He had never been that cold in his life. It was cold for the Tulsa players as well but that weather was more than the UNT team could overcome. They simply had not had to play football in that kind of cold and succumbed to it. They lost 17-6.

North Texas was 8-1 and again were the Missouri Valley Conference Champions. The last game of the season was against Drake University. The Monday of that week, the University of North Texas was officially invited to play in the Sun Bowl game in recognition of the excellent season they had turned in. Drake caught them at absolutely the wrong time as UNT was rolling and riding high. They steamrolled Drake 65-2 to finish the season 9-1.

Dad remembered this time fondly as he was reflective of the journey they had taken. From that undefeated untied freshman team, they had traveled such a long way. Three years later, they had shattered the myth that blacks couldn't integrate with whites. He thought of that first day at the stadium; he thought of all the hostile stadiums and teams they had gone up against and defeated. He thought of his teammates, this band of brothers who went through so much together. The Bald Eagles, Dad knew then that these guys had a bond that would never be broken. They had accepted the challenge and through their actions, created a new reality, a new norm. Together they have changed history and all have a better society because of it.

Chapter 8:
The Hunts

One of the greatest weekends for our family happened as Dad was enshrined in the Kansas City Chiefs Hall of Fame. There must have been seventy-five family members with us, we all drove in a Haynes convoy from Dallas to Kansas City for the ceremony.

It was one of the most elegant formal dinners I have ever seen. There was a celebrity golf tournament, we visited the Children's Hospital and just the camaraderie with the Hunt family and former Chiefs players was outstanding. This weekend is during the football season so that Sunday we took in the Chiefs game in the Hunt family suite at Arrowhead Stadium. The Chiefs owner Clark Hunt was very gracious. He continues to support Dad as he also attended the Doak Walker Awards ceremony with us as Dad received his Legends Award in 2022. When the Chiefs organization unveiled Dad's name on the rim of Arrowhead Stadium I was watching him closely. Dad was very moved. Almost brought to tears but with a satisfaction and appreciation on his face. He had the look of contentment and peace. I remember wondering exactly what he was thinking at that moment. I imagined that he was reliving some of the difficult days that he had been through. While there is much here in this work, I have left out many instances that Dad told me of that were too hateful or negative for print. He looked as if he was secretly thanking God for all the success and making it to that day. I believe he was quickly remembering some of the rugged practices the Texans/Chiefs used to have during training camp. I thought he was recalling those friends that didn't make it that far. I was just very happy for Dad that he was recognized for his elite performance on the field instead of being demonized for the positions he took in defense of our people. The Chiefs pulled out all the stops in honoring Dad. They are a classy organization, and have always been led by an awesome family. After the game we hit some of his old favorite spots including Gates Bar B Que. It was the ride home that was also eventful. This weekend was in late October and like most times we've been to Kansas City that time of year we were watching the weather closely. The Haynes convoy left Kansas City knowing we were trying to outrun a snowstorm, which caught up to us in Joplin Missouri. The police had closed the whole interstate and so we all checked into a hotel there and spent a couple days there in Joplin. It was great, we rented six rooms with the girls together and the men in others. Late that night Dad and I were sitting there discussing the wonderful weekend we had just experienced with the Chiefs when he became reflective as he often did. Even though he had told me of some of these things before he felt really good, we were safe from the snowstorm and I could see the satisfaction and twinkle in his eyes as he started to tell me how his relationship with the Hunt's came to be.

The times were different back then; the NFL did not hold its draft in April like it does now. There was about a month between UNT's last regular season game against Drake and the bowl game. This is the time Dad was going to have to decide the direction his life would take, going forward. He had already been drafted by the Pittsburgh Steelers of the NFL. He was also talking to the Winnipeg Blue Bombers of the Canadian League, as some black players of that time went that route to escape the Jim Crow attitudes and built in racism that was dominant here. Canada didn't have segregation and its people seemed above needing others to know that they hate them. After what Dad had just gone through for four years in college, I know that was appealing to him. Dad even flew to Winnipeg and met with them during the dead time before the bowl game. The NFL was there and had a few black players but at that time; there were still many of its teams that didn't have a single one. They were dragging their feet on integration as I imagine they had to go at a pace the public could handle. The Pittsburgh Steelers sent the legendary quarterback Bobby Layne and Head Coach Buddy Parker to the house in Dallas to convince Abner to join the Steelers.

There also was a new league, the AFL which was founded by a man from Dallas, Lamar Hunt. Mr. Hunt was a fair man whom Dad always called a great human being — a creative man whose business model for his league included bringing in more black players, particularly those from traditionally black universities. While the NFL at the time had a few blacks sprinkled across a few teams, they completely ignored all the players from the HBCUs.

The Dallas Texans/Kansas City Chiefs profited greatly from this approach as Buck Buchanan and Otis Taylor were but two examples. Hall of Fame players who came from the traditionally black universities. Mr. Hunt had spotted this untapped gusher of talent before his peers, increasing the talent level of his new league by leaps and bounds. Dad said that with Mr. Lamar Hunt, it was never about skin color, only ability.

As they talked together more and more, Dad could see Mr. Hunt was resolute in his intention to not only allow black players, but to encourage blacks in his league. He intended to break down a door that had only been cracked open a little by the NFL. Although he was the founder of the league, Mr. Hunt would also be the owner of the franchise in Dallas. Dad thought this was a perfect situation for him. He would be able to fulfill his dream of playing professional football a mere three blocks away from his family home. Dad and Mr. Hunt reached an agreement and, being the kind of man he was, Mr. Hunt insisted on being at the Sun Bowl game to sign Dad immediately after his last collegiate game. I've been told about all this since childhood but this night Dad was remembering teammates that had passed away. I know he was feeling grateful and blessed as he looked back at what brought us all to Kansas City, the life and career he had. I think he was amazed himself at all he had been through and survived. Segregation was real, some of the individuals who were against integration and against black people having decent lives were very serious. I also think Dad was aware that at some point in the future he wouldn't be able to tell his story and he was making sure that someone else could. He was content and fulfilled as he relived those days that changed so much.

Mr. Hunt was a vigorous man who knew what he was after so they had a great time with it all and Dad signed his first professional contract right there in El Paso under the goal post of the Sun Bowl.

During that month between the bowl game and the regular season finale, Dad and his father spent a lot of time discussing his options. Lamar Hunt and the Dallas Texans which would later become the Kansas City Chiefs, were the right choice. The fact that the team would play its home games at the Cotton Bowl, in the same neighborhood where Dad went to high school was a tremendous bonus.

PapaDad thought a lot of Mr. Hunt and his family and that carried a lot of weight in the Haynes home. Lamar's father was the legendary Texas oilman H.L. Hunt. Being from Dallas, both PapaDad and Abner knew of the Hunt family before all this ever came up as H.L. Hunt was regularly covered by the media of the day. This was a perfect setup.

The American Football League eventually merged with the NFL, and its teams formed the basis of what is now the AFC within the NFL. The AFL was all Lamar Hunt's idea. After continually being denied an expansion team by the NFL, it is said that Lamar sketched on a napkin during a plane flight the original plans for the AFL. Lamar had friends in this endeavor. He had assembled like-minded businessmen from across the country who had the courage and resources to challenge the NFL.

Barron Hilton Of Hilton Hotels in Los Angeles with the San Diego Chargers, Bud Adams in Houston with the Oilers, Billy

Sullivan in Boston whose team became the New England Patriots, Ralph Wilson in Buffalo with the Bills, Harry Wisner in New York with the Jets and Bob Howsam in Denver with the Broncos. These men were the pioneers who opened up a whole new world of football that black athletes could participate in and excel at. All these men were amongst the pioneers of the AFL and are widely recognized for their contributions to the great game of football that we all enjoy now. The NFL has been such a great organization through the years. It adapted and evolved right along with our country and has changed the lives of many families by now, but when Dad came through, it was not as welcoming as today.

Lamar Hunt was a passionate football man as well as being a great human being. He was only 27 years old when they all started out in that first season of the AFL. I first met Mr. Hunt at a pro game in Dallas. I was with my Dad; the Chiefs were not playing in this game and as I can recall we were all standing in the parking lot of the team's hotel that was playing. I was so young; I don't recall who was even playing that game. I know the Minnesota Vikings were there, but I do remember Mr. Lamar Hunt. He had such a commanding presence about himself that I always felt honored just to talk to him. I had an interest in business at a young age so as Dad would tell me about Lamar and H.L. Hunt, it really fascinated me that he knew men like this. We were near where the Anatole Hotel sits today in Dallas and Mr. Hunt took time to talk to me. He asked me all kinds of questions and made me feel like he cared about me. When I was talking to him, it seemed I had his undivided attention. He left me with the impression that he was really interested in what I was talking about and my point of view. I remember knowing who he was because Dad had already told me many stories and episodes and I always thought of Mr. Hunt as a great ally and friend of our family. Sure, he wasn't perfect and later the business of football caused them problems, but I know my Dad loved him and the success they enjoyed together formed the basis of their rock solid, lifelong relationship. The Hunt and Haynes family relationship has endured to this day.

My Dad always told me that Lamar Hunt and his father H.L. Hunt were the first mentors he ever had other than his own father. That is the way he thought of both of them. Dad appreciated the journey they took together. He recognized the way the Hunts accepted him and appreciated the way they treated him in that time of racial strife. He valued the way they would talk to him about life and all kinds of subjects and issues that didn't have anything to do with football. Lamar eventually became one of the most admired and respected people in the history of pro football. His innovative approaches and strategies helped the league thrive and grow into the juggernaut it is today. Dad's thought was that Lamar was the driving force that helped open up professional sports to black athletes. Mr. Hunt knew there was a wealth of talent going unused due to the fact there weren't enough professional teams. Lamar was a marketing genius whose vision benefited all.

Dad told me a lot about Lamar's father, H.L. Hunt over the years. I never met him but read and heard a lot about him when I was younger. I'm pretty sure that to Dad, one of the most impressive things about the relationship that he enjoyed with the

Hunt family was that they had one at all. This was a wealthy man who didn't have to associate with anyone. They were unusual people, who could have a real relationship with a young black man in the early 1960s.

I read at one point that Haroldson Lafayette Hunt was four times richer than the Rockefellers but despite his vast wealth, he was a famously frugal man. Dad used to tell me that he would sometimes park three blocks away from his destination to save the 50-cent parking fee. He cut his own hair and brought a sack lunch with him to work.

He was a man of bold convictions who believed in his own ways of doing things. His interests included real estate, cattle, and timber, but oil is what propelled his fortune. He was one of the pioneers of the legendary East Texas oil fields.

Dad always appreciated the elder Mr. Hunt's desire to bring him along. He would take Dad to lunch and was always talking to him about things that he had not heard about from other people. Mr. H.L. Hunt was authentic and was concerned, he didn't want Dad to get tricked by some salesman or investment guy looking to prey on athletes.

Dad enjoyed his company immensely. He passed some of these ideas on to me and would tell me that he got them from H.L. Hunt. Mr. Hunt explained to Dad that in his belief, the American economic system will exaggerate, mislead and outright lie in order to get your money. The number one thing was to get your money. All other considerations were secondary to that. He gave Dad long lectures about being watchful and on the lookout for shoddy products or substandard service. In Mr. Hunt's view, the individual had a responsibility to get what they paid for; knowing the system may give it to you, but the system's first and most important goal is getting your money. Dad and his family knew whatever they knew and that was extensive. At the same time, it was enlightening for Dad to hear how a wealthy white man looked at and saw the same world. It was a joy for Dad to be around and spend time with Mr. Hunt. Dad knew he was blessed to hear these truths about life from a absolute warrior in the early 1960s, when segregation and exclusion were still the rule more than the exception.

While we were still snowed in there in Joplin, Dad told me again the story of the first time H.L. Hunt took him to lunch. They went to a well-known cafe in Dallas and Mr. Hunt ordered them two hamburgers and two glasses of water, that's all. Dad was 21 or 22 years old at the time. He would tell me he might have thought the man would go in and immediately order the most expensive thing on the menu but not Mr. Hunt. Dad was flabbergasted as the waitress brought the check and Mr. Hunt meticulously examined his bill to ensure he had not been overcharged. I mean Abner Haynes was a young superstar in Dallas sitting there with H.L. Hunt, maybe the wealthiest man in the state of Texas. Everyone in the restaurant knew who both of them were — they probably weren't going to overcharge him but Mr. Hunt believed in his system and lived by it. He then paid the bill and when the waitress brought his change, he just as carefully counted his change to the last penny. Both father and son taught Dad a lot during a time in his life when he was like a sponge taking in what he could from those he trusted.

After his playing career wrapped up, Dad became one of the first Black Sports Agents. At one time, he had amassed a client list of some 90 NFL and NBA players. The church had taught him many things, but I always believed the basis of his knowledge of the tactics of negotiating, the business of NFL contracts, the business of professional sports came from the Hunts.

Chapter 9:
The Pros

Dad's first and most memorable professional coach was the legendary Hank Stram. I knew Coach Stram myself and I must say he was a delightful man. He was the ideal coach for the situation and the times. Coach Stram used to say Dad was a franchise player before they talked about franchise players. My father talked to me so much over the years about this time in his life that again it almost seems like I was there. Coach Stram often had his two sons at practice, Stu and Dale who were a couple of Dad's best friends. There was a family atmosphere maintained within the Texans/Chiefs that allowed them all to thrive. Abner Haynes was the Rookie of the Year and the Player of the Year in that first season they spent together. The only player in the history of professional football to accomplish that feat. He led the entire AFL in touchdowns, rushing attempts and yards, yards-per-rush and all-purpose yards (including tops in punt and kickoff returns) his rookie year. He led the league again in rushing in 1961, and in 1962, he recorded another first — gaining over 1,000 yards for the first time in team history (1,049). Dad was a rookie in 1960, a time of unparalleled racial strife in our country and he needed a coach who could at least somewhat understand the plight of the black players.

Coach Stram provided a wealth of knowledge and information for Dad. He would always take the time to answer questions about life, the media, fans or whatever else. He and his wife, Phyllis were dear friends who provided a great example to the players in any number of areas. Dad spoke of missing them both as well as Mr. Hunt many times.

Dad told me countless times of scoring touchdowns and piling up statistics in a game they probably won, only to come home that evening to see on television black people being attacked by police dogs and shot with water cannons just for wanting to be treated fairly and having the nerve to protest injustice. The old level of hate was upped to overt physical attacks as the system attempted to maintain the old status quo and keep black people in their place. Remember Dad's father was Bishop Haynes — they had been leading and supporting black people his whole life. Everything and everyone were in a period of adjustment in this country, the NFL included. Dad found it next to impossible to fulfill what was wanted of him from some of the leaders of the time. The idea they put forward was that he was blessed to be a professional athlete, to be able to enjoy the perks and privileges that come with that. That he should just focus on his own interests and keep quiet about how we handle the rest of his people. He should simply ignore the abuse and mistreatment that he saw basically every evening on the news. Dad found that impossible to live with. Some branded him as a troublemaker, others thought of him as a rebel. I'm quite sure he is happy with the choices he made and the stances that he took in support of our people even though those stances or rocking the boat — so to speak — cost him in different ways.

Coach Stram was a great motivator and very good at communicating with young men, even a black one. He and Dad had a bond that transcended race. Dad knew that Coach Stram really cared for him as an individual and under his tutelage and leadership Dad became the first Black Captain of a professional football team, the AFL brought change with its game. With all they had on their plates to juggle, they maintained their honor and relationship through it all. Coach Stram was a steady hand in his support of Dad who could see the unenviable position he was often in.

Coach Stram's son Dale and I have been great friends for years. He fondly remembered the times he got to spend with Dad during the Texan/Chief years. Dale told a great story that Dad told him about his father. Dale said that Abner spoke vividly of the day in 1961 when members of the Dallas Texans team were assembled in the meeting room of the Central Expressway Texans office. It was the day that the team's roster would be cut down to its final members. It was not known, but prior to the meeting, several players had been let go, and their absence went unnoticed. Coach Stram, who was usually very punctual, arrived 5 minutes late, which added to the anxiety in the room. During this time, so many thoughts flowed through Abner's mind. "Would this meeting be his last with the team"? "If not, who would be cut from the team" "What does Coach want to tell us"? Coach Stram entered the room, he was, as always, dressed appropriately; wearing his monogrammed red Dallas Texans coaching shorts and white Texans shirt. Everyone in the room was silent, as Coach began to speak "Gentlemen, please look around at the faces of the men in this room". After nearly a minute, he continued by saying "You are all members of the 1961 Dallas Texans Family". "You have been chosen to represent the great city of Dallas, the Hunt organization, and me and my family". "At that moment I felt proud to have earned this man's trust", Abner said. "I believed in this man and his message", "I believed that he genuinely loved us and thought of us all as his family". "I wanted to win for this man, and at that moment, I knew that we would". The room erupted with excitement, we all hugged our nearest teammate, and no one cared what color he was. We were a team and most importantly we were a family.

Dad had a great group of guys for teammates with the Texans/Chiefs. He speaks often of the different men and I too have known many of them. E.J. Holub was from Texas Tech. He is a member of the College Football Hall of Fame and was as tough as nails. He was a western kind of man, always decked out in his boots and cowboy hat. Dad often said there was no one he'd rather have on his side during a fight as E.J. Holub. He was one of the nicest men I've ever met. I really respected his style and of course I was aware of the secret stories that Dad had told me over the years.

Sherrill Headrick was from TCU and was always ready to defend Dad on or off the field. Chris Burford and Frank Jackson were the wide receivers, great friends of Dad's and mine. There were so many who played pivotal roles in everything, but I'm mentioning some of those that I knew myself. Chris Burford is another member of the College Football Hall of Fame who graduated with honors from Stanford. Chris and Dad quickly became brothers. He broke another barrier silently as Chris invited and hosted Dad to dinner at his house. This was simply not done in 1960 in Dallas or probably most of the country. That was a line that wasn't crossed, blacks dining with whites. Chris was such a norm breaking advocate for Dad who helped move racial relations forward that Dad, some 50 years after they played together nominated Chris, a white guy, to the African-American Ethnic Sports Hall of Fame. John Gilliam was the team's center and as southern as they come. He was another teammate who would have none of it if anyone treated Dad with any disrespect. In fact, Dad told me the story of John Gilliam, who was from East Texas State University, Sherrill Headrick and him deciding to drive to San Diego to an AFL all-star game they were playing in. They were all free thinkers who wanted to see what would happen when white guys rode across the country with a black guy in the same car. Again in 1963 whites didn't do much of anything with a black person. Somewhere in Arizona, they were fatigued and stopped at a nice clean looking motel. The clerk informed the trio that Sherrill and John could indeed have rooms but because the other person was black he would have to find somewhere else to stay. The clerk had just said the wrong thing. At two in the morning, way out in some sleepy town in Arizona Sherrill Headrick was ready to defend Dad with his life. Make no mistake this was no acting job. Sherrill was not going to sit still while this clerk insulted his brother. Dad knew by this time in his life that escalating any situation would usually not work in the best interest of the black person involved. He was able to calm Sherrill down and they just moved on. They stopped at the next motel down the road and all three were welcomed to stay. They were all committed to each other and they were consistent with it at all times. Men you could count on who had a lifetime bond.

Another of my Dad's great friends and teammates was his quarterback The late Len Dawson who was from Purdue University. Len's son, Len Dawson Jr., and I have also been great friends for years as we have met at different Kansas City Chief events and discussed our Dads' careers and life for years. Len Jr. told me of some of the conversations he had with his father over the years and how he felt about my Dad. Len Jr's recollections of his Dad's thoughts are so powerful that I wanted to give life to some of our conversations.

Len Sr. related how when he arrived in Dallas in 1962, he had not started a game in a couple years due to injuries. His skills as a quarterback had eroded somewhat due to missed playing time. Lamar Hunt had traded Cotton Davidson, who was the Texans starting quarterback the previous two years, to Oakland. Len knew he had a very tough road ahead of him and he needed a lot of help. Len told his son that fortunately he had a guy in his backfield from North Texas State University by the name of Abner Haynes. In 1960 Abner was drafted by the Dallas Texans, he was named the Rookie of the Year and then voted MVP of the league. I do not think that had ever happened before or after, in either the AFL or NFL he would tell Len Jr.

"You just do not understand the pressure this took off my shoulders as a quarterback having him in my backfield. He was the first all-around offensive weapon in professional football. He could do it all with ease, block, run the ball, catch the ball out of the backfield, or as a wide receiver, plus he ran back our punts and kickoffs". According to Len Dawson, Abner Haynes was the total package.

Len Jr. would tell me often how his Dad felt, he told me many times how Len Dawson thought Abner was ahead of his time in professional football and in history, especially when you remember what was going on in our country during the 1960's. Black players were just integrating into the sport of pro football.

Len Sr. went on to say "It seemed like there was a target on Abner's back every game coming from the opposing players and their fans. It made no difference to our team whether he was black or white, because his talent always kept him one step ahead of all opponents. He was a very instrumental part in the Dallas Texans winning the 1962 AFL Championship". Len developed into a great quarterback, who also went on to become a fixture in Kansas City as a sports broadcaster.

Being that the AFL was new, it attempted different ways to grow the league. As I stated earlier, Lamar Hunt was a genius at marketing. At this time, there were many larger cities in our country that still did not have a professional football team. Mr. Hunt of course recognized this, so he had the Texans play a series of exhibition games in cities without teams.

Dad told a great story about this time in history. He told me of this incident one day when we had done what we did at least once a year, we left the city of Dallas to go out to our ranch. It was a special mission we were on that day. One of Dad's favorite activities to do was when we would go to a fish farm near the ranch to restock our lake. It was so refreshing and fun to see their operation. All the new life being brought along in all their different ponds We'd get to examine the different varieties and strains of fish they were breeding. We'd have to decide do we want fingerlings or adults. We would always buy fathead minnows for the fish to eat. They swim slow yet reproduce fast. It was just such a peaceful and tranquil way to spend a day so we loved to go there. Then it would be up to us to get the new fish to the lake where we would feed them and defend them from predators until they were ready for harvest. We got so much joy from having fresh clean fish to give away to family and friends. That's what makes the effort so much worth it. Our fish are free of mercury and benzene and all the other pollutants that seem to be in commercial fish as our lake is fed by an underground spring.

The Texans were in Little Rock Arkansas to play the Denver Broncos in a game that brought much excitement to fans who normally didn't have pro football in their hometown. Everything seemed to be going along as usual until the team arrived at a posh downtown hotel. You see, this was 1961 and the state of Arkansas did not allow blacks in "white" hotels. Dad recalls that none of the players liked it. white or black. They were a team and this was all sprung on them at the last moment, so what could they do. Coach Stram was greatly distressed at having to tell the three black players on the team to remain on the bus. There was almost an open revolt by the white players as they were a family, a team in their minds. They weren't going to sit idly by as anyone demeaned or insulted their teammates. His white brothers were whooping and hollering, waving and shouting as the bus continued on straight to where they would stay. In short order, they recognized they had entered the black part of town and shortly got to the "black hotel". They took a little rest and got up later to look around a bit. It was Dad's road roommate, the great Clem Daniels, who would later go on to star for the Oakland Raiders with him as they decided to just get a little air and maybe some dinner. As soon as they came out of their room, they heard noises coming from downstairs. The pair followed the noise as it got louder and louder until they came upon a sort of ballroom at the hotel. They couldn't believe their eyes. The room was packed with people. Dad looked to his right and there was Leroy Cooper, the great jazz saxophonist going off with his horn. Then a familiar voice started crooning to his left; he then turned around and made eye contact with the legendary Ray Charles. They told Ray the guys were there and he stopped the show to introduce them.

This game had been big news in Little Rock so the crowd was very excited to get a chance to see these young professional athletes. It was still new, the system allowing black men to attain that level of success as black Americans knew all too well. Black people everywhere rooted for them in hopes of a better future for us all. What started out as a sort of negative as once again the issue of race had to rear its head became a wonderful night. They had a great time.

Dad's friend Chris Burford, called over to the hotel wanting to check on how he was doing. They came and got Dad from the show to answer the phone and Chris heard the music in the background as they talked. He was mad as heck. Chris kept demanding to know what they had going on at their hotel. Dad told him and had the staff give him directions to the hotel and in short order Chris and most of the rest of the white players had come over to the black hotel. They all had a great time together. Blacks and whites together like it should be just relaxing, enjoying great music and each other.

My Father could tell such compelling stories of things that didn't have anything to do with football. We talked so much, traveled so many miles together, but one of his football stories was so funny I've never forgotten it. The Texans were in Boston to play the Patriots. A little background on this. The first time I remember Dad relating this story to me, we had company with us. Dad was a very successful Sports Agent at this time. He was based in Houston so we made the drive between Dallas and Houston at least once a week. Our Circle H Ranch was in between the two cities so we could stop and take a break out in the country either coming or going. Needless to say, we always had our fishing gear in the back of the van. Well on this particular trip we had two of Dad's former clients with us. Ron Shanklin and Glen Holloway. These were two great men. Ron was from Amarillo, Texas, where he was a state champion in the 400 meters in high school. He went on to star in the NFL as an All-Pro wide receiver of the Pittsburgh Steelers. In one of his seasons Ronnie led the entire NFL with an average 23.7 yards per catch. He was one of my father's closest confidants for many years. They just had a special chemistry and bond. We called him Shank, Ronnie was a joy to be around. He was a funny guy who was full of stories himself. Like us, Shank loved to fish. He knew about more great fishing spots than anyone. I always remember a couple different times we all drove to Amarillo with Shank as he and his brother operated a nightclub there. Shank was like the mayor in Amarillo. Everyone knew him and our money was no good there. Whatever you needed Shank had someone who could provide.

Due to how the years shook out, of all the ex-players and wealthy businessmen my father introduced me to over the years there was a core group of accomplished men who were special to him. Hurles Scales was a hard-hitting defensive back for the St. Louis Cardinals who had 4.3 speed. Jean Fugett was a great athlete but also a very intelligent and accomplished attorney. Because of their close relationships with each other I knew all of these men basically my whole life. Glen Holloway was from Corpus Christi Texas, the other end of the state from Amarillo. He was an outstanding athlete as an offensive guard who was drafted by and became a captain of the Chicago Bears. He was named to the NFL's All-Rookie Team and was the first recipient of the Brian Piccolo Award. Glen was a composed and calm man. A very smart guy, he was very loyal to my Dad as he had a successful pro career himself under Dad's guidance. Glen was easy to talk to and helped us recruit offensive linemen for our agency. We had done our business in Houston and were heading back home when Shank brought up this particular game that Dad played in against the Patriots. Dad had so many unique experiences and memories to sort through, I could always tell, as

I could see the light of recollection come over his face as he began to tell me the story. Dad said the game was very competitive. The Texans/Chiefs were down 14-0 to the Patriots when Dad's great friend Chris Burford started taking over the game from the wide receiver position. They couldn't contain Chris as the Texans rode that advantage to tie the game. With time running out the Texans/Chiefs were down 28-21, but were on the Patriots goal line with a chance to tie the game and send it to overtime. It appeared to all that a final play had been run and that time had run out and the Patriots won, but the team's fans had run onto the field in celebration of victory prematurely and interfered in the Texans last play. After a conference of the officials, it was decided that the Texans/Chiefs would get a redo. One last play to make up for the fans disrupting the previous play. You see, this is 1961, so much had happened in these games over the years to help professional football evolve into the game we all know today. The exuberance of the Patriots fans was something the rules of the game had not taken into account at that time. After foiling the previous Texans play by running onto the field, the fans were lined up all along the playing field, crowded around the end zone maybe ten rows deep as the Texans would run a final play from the goal line. There was no security or anything controlling people's access to just walk on the field back in those days. Dad went on explaining how they lined up for the last play. It was going to be a fade to Chris Burford who was six feet four inches against the five-foot nine cornerback who he had been abusing the whole game. Before they even snapped the ball, he saw one fan walk through the back of the end zone in total street clothes and line up as a linebacker. He was in his stance just like one of the players. The Patriots had an extra defender. As the play unfolded this sneaky fan rolled to the right, flowing right along with the play and batted the ball to the ground before Chris could catch it. The frenzied fans stormed the field and no one in charge had even noticed what the overexcited fan had done as an extra defender. The Texans/Chiefs lost 28-21. After Dad told me this hilarious episode, I later saw an actual video of the play.

The 1962 season was very successful for the Dallas Texans. They met the Houston Oilers for the AFL Championship at Jeppesen Stadium in Houston. At the time, it was the longest game in the history of pro football. A double overtime thriller in which Dad scored two touchdowns. The Texans won 20-17 and following that successful season, the team moved to Kansas City and became the Chiefs.

Locker room celebration after the 1962 Championship

One of the things Abner Haynes is best known for happened in 1965. He had been selected to play in the AFL All-Star game, which would be played in New Orleans. New Orleans was another city that had no professional football team. The AFL was growing its brand and getting exposure by ensuring it held games in these cities which had no team of their own to root for. Lamar Hunt was a shrewd businessman. There were a number of black players on each All-Star team. From the instant they landed at the airport, it seemed the city of New Orleans was determined to show them they were not welcomed.

On another trip. The great offensive tackle of the Dallas Cowboys, the late Rayfield Wright was with us. Rayfield was from Griffin, Georgia. We called him Big Cat, because he was as quick as a cat despite his imposing size. A Hall of Famer who was an absolute monster on the field. Off the field, however, he was different. Calm and thoughtful, another very smart man, we were very tight. Rayfield loved my Dad, as Abner steered him through his professional career as his agent. I can recall staying with Rayfield and his wife a couple weeks one summer at their house in Dallas, when I was around 12 years old. My brother Abner Jr. and I had a great time with them and our bond lasted from that time. Rayfield told me wonderful stories of his mother and grandmother raising him and his time growing up in Georgia. He was a regular at Dad's house and also helped us recruit offensive and defensive lineman for the agency. Well, Rayfield was riding with us on this road trip. We had gone down to the gulf coast south of Houston to Seabrook where you could buy wholesale seafood right off the boat. We'd bring fresh crab, shrimp and oysters packed in ice back home to Dallas. I would always be enthralled just to hear the two of them talk and tell stories of life and football. We were riding up Interstate 45 shucking and eating fresh oysters as Rayfield asked Dad about the boycott in New Orleans. I had heard Dad speak of this but not with a grown person's perspective like this day.

Dad began telling Rayfield and I about that All Star game in New Orleans. Dad's friend, Clem Daniels had already been traded to the Oakland Raiders and had an outstanding season that year. Clem, who was from McKinney, Texas just north of Dallas was also selected for the game and had come home first so that he and Dad could fly into New Orleans together. The two of them stood there outside the airport hailing taxi after taxi. Of course, this was 1965 — no black men were allowed to be taxi drivers or much of anything in New Orleans. They stood there as the cab drivers would zoom right by them to pick up a white passenger who may not have even signaled them yet. After a while of this and seeing what was happening, they finally found a black man with a car whom they paid to take them to the team's hotel.

Upon arriving at the hotel, Dad was confronted by a contingent of players from the Buffalo Bills. They didn't know anything about what Dad and Clem had just gone through with the taxi drivers, but each began to tell him of the treatment they were receiving. They had been refused service at several restaurants there in New Orleans and along with the denied service were peppered with ethnic and racial slurs.

Dad was concerned for his friends, as all the players knew each other despite being on different teams, and this was turning out to be a very hostile situation for all of them. The group of players met there in the lobby for a time before Ernie Ladd, who later became a great pro wrestler who was 6 '9 inches tall, Cookie Gilchrist, Clem Daniels and Dad decided to go up to his room to discuss the situation more privately. They didn't want to incite the players any more than the people of New Orleans had already done. The younger readers wouldn't know but most nice hotels or office buildings in 1965 had elevator operators; that was actually a job. This hotel had an elevator operator and as Dad and the other three players boarded the elevator along with a white guest, the elevator operator turned around, looked at them and said in a loud and commanding voice, "You four monkeys, get in the back". It was all Dad could do to keep Ernie Ladd from tearing the guy apart right there on the spot. He had said a foolish thing to the wrong men, but he felt comfortable enough in New Orleans to say it. They realized of course, they were in Louisiana in 1965, and although they have great food there, there was no way a black person was going to do anything to a white person without coming out with the short end of the stick. That's just the way it was back then. After this elevator incident, the players felt like there was no need to hold back anything.

The accommodations and being separated in Little Rock was one thing, but no one in Little Rock disrespected any players. They were not treated like they were animals, like what went on in New Orleans. The treatment they received from a variety of individuals and businesses was more than any of them could stomach. They would then trot out onto the field to entertain these same people who made a point to treat them as dirt or even less than human.

What was also interesting about all of this was the reactions of some of the white All-Star players. Jack Kemp was the quarterback of the Buffalo Bills who went on to distinguish himself in service to our country and rose up to be Housing Secretary in the Bush Administration. After he heard the accounts of what the black All-Stars had gone through, he was livid. He demanded that they include him in any meetings about what they would do and made it clear that they were all in this together.

Dad's great friend and Texans teammate Jerry Mays was very upset as well. They were more than just pro teammates. Jerry was also from Dallas. His family owned a big construction company. Their lives had followed similar paths. Both of them were products of Dallas high schools, went to college close to home - Jerry went to SMU - and they both played professionally in their own hometown. Jerry wasn't so much the vocal leader, but he let Dad know that whatever they decided to do, he was with them 100 percent. Dad told us that until they all left New Orleans, Jerry Mays would not leave his side.

These were men who stood out amongst their peers as All Stars; they were not intimidated. They held a meeting that included many of the white players in the game and decided unanimously to boycott the game. All of them decided to stick together for better or worse, but they would not go out and put on an exhibition in a city that went out of its way to belittle them like New Orleans did.

These were grown men with wives and children at home. Men who wanted a better future for their own kids and the country as a whole. My Dad was fighting for something the whole time that was greater than football. Dignity, respect, a fair chance for all. It was much more than simply playing a game or entertaining people. This was something that they simply couldn't tolerate and feel good about themselves. Unfortunately, this was the first boycott of a city by any sporting event in history. It was not popular with everyone and even some of the black players thought they should just keep their mouths shut and get their money. The leaders however chose to not bow to the hate and ignorance, and to the AFL's credit, they understood what the black players were going through and moved the game to Houston.

This was a pivotal moment for Dad. Seeing the hate and bigotry was nothing new for descendants of slaves — what Dad remembered most is just like that freshman season at North Texas, his white teammates had his back. This was true because they were brothers who had worked, sweated, won and grew together. They weren't concerned with the color of each other's skin, only that some of their brothers were being attacked and they stood up against it, together. He saw progress in the country through them and although the road to fairness and equality was a difficult one, Dad felt that we all had come a long way and he believed in the future of our country and its people walking through this life together.

Chapter 10:
The Zale Influence

The other mentor that was so instrumental in Dad's life and professional development was another local Dallas guy. Mr. Donald Zale was one of Dad's biggest fans. His father M.B. Zale was a Jewish man who immigrated from eastern Europe and in time opened a jewelry store in Wichita Falls Texas. His first store was not altogether successful. It was in Graham Texas and the Ku Klux Klan was against him due to the fact that he was Jewish. They burned the store to the ground and told him in no uncertain terms to get out of town, which the elder Mr. Zale did. What a true story for sticking with your dreams, what an example of being determined and not giving up. Together the Zale family starting from scratch built an absolute juggernaut of a company. The Zale way proved wildly successful as in time they became the largest jewelry company in the world. The Zale Corporation had over 20,000 employees at its peak.

Mr. Donald Zale was a delightful man. A graduate of Texas A&M University, Mr. Zale was perhaps the most polished and smooth person I have ever known. I always felt a little smarter after spending time with him. Dad called him D.Z. Some of Dad's favorite stories to tell me were of their legendary hunting trips together. The Zale's had a huge ranch down in South Texas. They would all go down for a little relaxation and time away from the pressure cooker that was being in the diamond business. Dad always was watching those around him, he passed that on to me as well. He would tell me about Mr. Zale, how he enjoyed his comfort. They would be out in the middle of nowhere hunting deer, but Mr. Zale had a heater in the deer blind and nice comfortable chairs. He was out hunting in the rugged land of South Texas but he had his hot coffee and fine food along with him. He really enjoyed the outdoors and taught Dad how to skin and butcher his deer. We have lots of family stories about the two of them. Mr. Zale was a very compassionate man who was committed to doing what was right and fair. Many people don't know, but it was the Zale family that almost single handedly came up with the idea of credit. That started back in Wichita Falls, which had a large Air Force base. Mr. M.B. Zale wanted to make it easier for the military members to buy his watches. He provided excellent customer service by letting the airmen buy watches with installment payments of 2 dollars a week. Zale's was the first company that would extend credit to black people. What a track record this family had. Dad really respected them, after the racial animosity that Dad had lived through up to that point, integrating Texas universities, boycotts, mistreatment and blackballing in the pros. I am sure it was a refreshing and invigorating thing to find this Jewish family that didn't harbor a secret hatred of him due to the color of his skin. Dad retired earlier than he had to from professional football because he saw the opportunity to learn from and be trained in business by the

Zale family. Mr. Zale had explained to Dad that he didn't want to just give him a job but rather he was going to have Dad work in all the different departments of the company in order to be well- trained, knowledgeable officer of the company.

Dad continued learning and absorbing the business until he rose to become the first black corporate officer in the history of the Zale Corporation. The incident that put him over the top at Zale's happened in Atlanta Georgia. Zale's was expanding. They were buying other companies and expanding into different industries. They had purchased a shoe company based there in Atlanta. That company's employees were striking, picketing and protesting, not against the shoe company, but rather in front of Zale's jewelry stores in Atlanta once they found out about the sale and who was the new parent company. M.B. Zale had built his company from the beginning with a careful eye on customer service. He famously refused to raise his prices and was almost obsessed with the customer's satisfaction. He was not about to stand by and watch protest and calamity happening in front of a Zale store. Now, it happens that most of these unhappy employees were black. Being that all this is happening in Atlanta, that's not so surprising. This is the late 1960's or early 1970's so the previous owner of the shoe company was more than likely not generous with pay or benefits, but as soon as the employees found out it was Zale's that bought them out, they thought they may get better working conditions and indeed they did get a reaction all the way back in Dallas. M.B. and Donald Zale thought Dad was ready to handle and solve a challenge like this so they sent Abner Haynes to Atlanta to solve it all. Dad told me they sent him but not with any specific instructions. Dad was charged with solving it. Getting everyone involved what they needed and resolving the standoff. He would have to assess the lay of the land when he got there and come up with a solution to get these people back working, and to get those protest out from in front of Zale's stores. Dad did just that; he resolved it all to everyone's satisfaction. The teaching and training that Mr. Zale sent Abner through had paid off. His Zale's career rocketed upward after that and our families remained tight all these years later. By the time I was a teenager the two of them worked so well together that it was just special. Dad loved Mr. Donald Zale because of the way he treated him, because of the kind of man he was. He loved Mr. Zale for all they did for him but also for the times they did it in. Dad often remarked to me concerning the way Zale's treated their employees. They were amongst the first companies to introduce a profit-sharing plan for their employees. There were many companies that in the late 1960's wouldn't allow a black man to be much past a janitor, if they employed a black person at all. The Zale family were just great people who were ahead of their time. It was always going to be an interesting experience wherever we met Mr. Zale somewhere. We often went sailing on his boat on Lake Ray Hubbard near Dallas. It was more a sailing yacht; he could let the wind propel it but it also certainly had engines. Mr. Zale enjoyed showing me how everything worked and, of course, anything you may have wanted for refreshments was on board. Mr. Zale's wife Barbara was a great lady as well, she always felt better when D.Z. went with us because she knew he would be safe. I used to love the experience when he would take us to lunch or dinner at one of his preferred spots. He was a larger-than-life personality to me. I had never seen a restaurant's employees act the way they did when Mr. Zale was around. Of course, they already knew who he was and they acted accordingly. I never ate a meal with him when he didn't have half the room to himself and he would just offer you everything on the menu. He was a fun guy to be around for me, that's for sure. Mr. Zale has passed away, but he will be forever remembered for his kindness and generosity to those less fortunate. RIP

Epilogue

After his successful playing career which included learning about the business of football, the contracts and philosophy. After his ultra successful years learning and growing as a Businessman/Executive with the Zale Corporation, my Dad became one of the first Black Sports Agents. At one point, Dad was the Agent for the entire vaunted Steel Curtain defensive line of the Pittsburgh Steelers. Three of four of them were from Texas with Joe Greene even attending the same groundbreaking university UNT. Dad presided over the deal of the NFL's first free agent. Jean Fugett, the great tight end of the Dallas Cowboys who is one of Dad's greatest friends and business partners went to the Washington Redskins without the Cowboys receiving any compensation. Dad at one time was the representative of over 80 NFL, NBA and Track & Field athletes.

Abner Haynes & Associates (left clockwise), Beverly Isaiah-Bermudez, K. David Haynes, Guadalupe Gonzalez and Abner Haynes

During the time I served as the National Recruiter for Abner Haynes & Associates, we had many successes. Dad and I spent lots of time together. We drove to many places, as he was usually avoiding getting on planes unless circumstances dictated. We both enjoyed the variety of driving instead of flying, seeing the country, stopping where we wanted. It was different back then. Being on the road was much safer than it is now.

Abner Haynes, King David Haynes

We'd take our fishing poles with us and just have great times. These were some of the greatest trips and experiences of my life. We would talk and talk about all kinds of subjects as we passed the time. This is why he knew I could write this book.

Dad would like to speak to his younger fans as well. He wanted to remind them of the importance of education and hard work. He had always been a guy of great character and knew the importance of standing for and being committed to that which you believe in. There is nothing more important than your education. To the young athletes coming up, believe in yourself, put in your hard work. Dad knew that you can make your dreams come true through dedication and commitment. In the beginning, no one knew who he was but through perseverance, faith and unwavering determination, he was able to achieve his goals and so can you.

Dad was a first in so many areas, a hero, trailblazer and pioneer who when opportunity knocked was ready with preparation. His talent — I'm told — was undeniable, but his career did suffer due to the times he lived through. Integration and equality were certainly not popular with everyone. Many wanted things to remain as they had always been. Some officials branded him a troublemaker for advocating for his people. Others wanted him silenced, blackballed even for rocking the boat of racial inequity that was the norm in the 1960's. How dare he complain about the way black people were mistreated.

Dad felt good about the stands he took and never regretted the choices he made. He was helped along this path by his parents and also the people of Denton, Dallas, Kansas City and Houston in particular. They all felt hope and optimism for their own children's prospects because Dad and his teammates overcame so many obstacles together. The overwhelming success of the great experiment of integration allowed other schools, companies, organizations, and individuals to rethink the policies of exclusion, to openly accept blacks in their universities and organizations without the sky falling. Dad paved the way of race integration for so many to follow, so that this world could be a better place by overcoming so much adversity with hard work, an infectious spirit and unwavering commitment. Dad and I felt that if his story could inspire even a few people to adjust their way of thinking regarding fairness, opportunity and inclusion, this book would have achieved one of its goals. Truth and honesty always work best. Dad was content, he gave his all, he stayed away from trouble and he lived a remarkably successful life. He is at peace and wanted to give one last thanks to all of his fans

About The Author

King David is Abner Haynes' son who has worked closest with him through the years. He is an Author, Voice Actor and tireless advocate for those recovering from addictions.

King David's debut book, "A Lame Man Healed: How the Son of a Football Star Overcame Addiction Through Faith," is a true story about how faith in God and Jesus Christ saved him from the strongholds of addiction. He believes there are two reasons why the Holy Spirit compelled him to tell his story. Through his book, King David wants to be a beacon of hope for all types of addicts and to provide comfort and optimism for an addict's family and friends who suffer as well. Here is the link to the book: https://a.co/d/0VWscv2

Prior to writing A Lame Man Healed, he founded Prodigal Son Re-Entry Ministry and served as its Chief Operating Officer (CEO). The non-profit organization is tax-exempt and dedicated to facilitating programs that encourage a successful transition from addiction and incarceration to a productive life that includes a combination of support services, counseling, education, and job training.

Made in the USA
Middletown, DE
01 July 2025